Landscape of Desire

Landscape of Desire

Partial Stories of the Medieval Scandinavian World

Gillian R. Overing and Marijane Osborn

University of Minnesota Press

Minneapolis

London

Figures 1, 2, 3, and 7 were prepared by Craig Hillis, principal artist, University of California—Davis Illustration Services. Used with permission of the map-maker. Figure 19 used with permission of the Central Bank of Iceland.

Plate 1, taken by Randolph Swearer, used with permission of the photographer.

An earlier version of "Reinventing Beowulf's Voyage to Denmark" was published in *Old English Newsletter* 21, no. 2 (Spring 1988): 30–39. Reprinted here in revised form with permission.

Published by the University of Minnesota Press
2037 University Avenue Southeast, Minneapolis, MN 55455–3092

Printed in the United States of America on acid-free paper

Library of Congress Cataloging-in-Publication Data
Overing, Gillian R., 1952–
    Landscape of desire : partial stories of the medieval Scandinavian world / Gillian R. Overing and Marijane Osborn.
        p.   cm.
    Includes bibliographical references (p.   ) and index.
    ISBN 0-8166-2374-0 (hc : acid-free).   —   ISBN 0-8166-2375-9 (pb : acid-free)
    1. Beowulf.   2. Literature, Comparative—English (Old) and Scandinavian.   3. Literature, Comparative—Scandinavian and English (Old).   4. Overing, Gillian R., 1952–   —Journeys—Scandinavia.
    5. Osborn, Marijane—Journeys—Scandinavia.   6. Epic poetry, English (Old)—History and criticism.   7. Geography, Medieval, in literature.
    8. Literary landmarks—Scandinavia.   9. Scandinavia—In literature.
    10. Landscape in literature.   I. Osborn, Marijane.   II. Title.
PR1587.S28095   1994
829'.09—dc20   93-32773

The University of Minnesota is an equal-opportunity educator and employer.

For Rose Overing and Morgan Allen

The perceptions of any people wash over the land, leaving ideas hung up in the brush, like pieces of damp paper to be collected and deciphered. No one can tell the whole story.

Barry Lopez
Arctic Dreams

Space that has been seized upon by the imagination cannot remain indifferent space subject to the measures and estimates of the surveyor. It has been lived in, not in its positivity, but with all the partiality of the imagination.

Gaston Bachelard
The Poetics of Space

She comes out of herself to go to the other, a traveler in unexplored places; she does not refuse, she approaches, not to do away with the space between, but to see it, to experience what she is not, what she is, what she can do.

Hélène Cixous and Catherine Clément
The Newly Born Woman

Contents

Acknowledgments

❖

We would like to thank our respective institutions for their financial support: Wake Forest University and the University of California at Davis have generously and enthusiastically supported this project by granting both funding and research leave time. Peter Bolwig, captain of the *Galadriel*, and first mate Kristian Fabricius deserve our warmest gratitude for their indefatigable energy and good humor. We thank Carol Martin for leading us to the *Galadriel*; Ole Crumlin-Pedersen, director of the Viking Ship Museum in Roskilde, Denmark, for giving us invaluable assistance and information; and our mapmaker, Craig Hillis.

Many have contributed directly and indirectly to the successful completion of our journeys and to the making of this book. Some have provided emotional, intellectual, or material support, while others have given us all three. We thank Kristín Arngrimsdóttir, Josephine Bloomfield, the Central Bank of Iceland (for the use of its logo), Jan Ekborg, the horses and riders of Fox Run Farm in High Point, North Carolina, Johann Hannesson, Gunnar Haraldsson, Bert Hedin, Rannveig Jónsdóttir, Sean O'Grady, and Randolph Swearer. Steve Ford has been characteristically gracious and steadfast throughout the many stages of this project.

Introduction

It is hard to say when, or more to our point, *where* this book began. It began in many places for varied reasons, and to write an introduction to it is to collect fragments from our past experience, and to discover the threads that might connect them to the present. We are, by profession, medievalists, leaning rather heavily toward Old English, and this we hold in common. The first place we hold in common is the north of England where we met: the fell country just south of the Lake District, the browner, bleaker cousin to Wordsworth's glorious landscapes. But it was some years before we explained to ourselves and to each other that this place was so powerful, before we understood that its shapes and colors were to haunt our personal lives and to influence our academic careers and interests.

We share a belief in the life of the past; its presence intrudes upon us. The past has never been dead, has always assumed a place in the present that we have both attempted to define in our work and to understand in our lives. We have come squarely up against the theoretical issues of historicizing fiction and fictionalizing history in our various attempts to "reinvent" the past, and this book is to a considerable extent a meditation on the problems and possibilities that arise in any present negotiation with the past.

In a collection of essays titled *Writing the Past in the Present*, a contemporary archaeologist tells this story:

We tell local inhabitants that the dun [*sic*] on the sea coast 200 m from their home is probably (almost certainly) Iron Age, 2000 years old. They will laugh and say, "Nonsense, that is the castle of the Clan Mackinnon, it was built as a defence against the Vikings." I laugh, but we are both right, our individual belief systems set that particular monument in a context which establishes where we are now. That past for the local community is an intricate part of their present. They identify with it far more than I do, as children they played hide-and-seek in it, their parents told them the story of its grim and mysterious past and their parents knew everything about the land, the name of every burn and hill. . . . Until we understand the nature of their version, how that past is a part of their present, we cannot dump our professional histories on their doorstep. (Mackay, in Baker and Thomas, 1990: 196–97)

We have many similar stories. We asked for directions at a gas station in Borgarnes north of Reykjavik, the town named after the home of the notorious viking Egil Skallagrimsson. We were looking for "Kveldulf's Head," the headland where the saga says that Egil's grandfather's coffin was washed ashore. The mechanic took us on a tour of several headlands, discussing other locals' theories but finally explaining why he was convinced of the accuracy of one in particular.

These stories suggest several principles that underlie and motivate our study of the past. One is our primary acknowledgment of the power and presence of place; we share places with the past, and we view the experience of place as a negotiative activity whereby we may extend, develop, or invent our dialogue with the past. Another principle is that the past consists in divergent stories told in the present, and a third is that our own histories and desires contribute to, sometimes dictate, the shape and purpose of those stories. We choose, consciously or not, how we will write history, and whether we will create it as same, other, or analogue.[1] Julian Thomas describes how no one approach can completely avoid the pitfalls of the others. We can re-create the past in our present image, or we can seek to recover its difference and so "de-legitimise the present" (Thomas, 1990: 20), and in either case we must accept that at some point we "simply write a story" (20). We can opt for an attempt at dialogue, or reconciliation between the two: "A history written as an Analogue is a story written in the present, which weaves together the traces of the past in a web of rationalization" (20). Although, as Thomas observes, this approach will not fully prevent the critic from taming, judging, or domesticating the past, the construction of history-as-analogue is one that we are consciously adopting in our own practice. Because all critics choose their version of the past on necessarily political and ideological grounds, Thomas concludes by advocating a vigilant attention to critical practice, thereby reflecting the archaeological variant of a view that is gaining currency in medieval studies in general. Allen J. Frantzen has most recently and cogently argued that medievalists should question the illusion of the neutrality of the skills of traditional medieval scholarship and contemporary criticism; both are products of a specific age and time. He casts medievalists' critical practice in terms of a dialogue between past and present, personal and professional, "in which we find another way of knowing ourselves and our predecessors, and of speaking their languages, as well as our own, in the conversation through which we know the Middle Ages" (Frantzen, 1991: 33).[2]

In a sense we have moved via fiction and history to a clearer understanding of our critical and personal practice. We began with a suspicion, and then a conviction, that "real" things mattered, held their own and their own existence—that the *Beowulf* poet, for example, might have seen such helmets and halls and places as he mentions in his poem, or that he knew in some measure of the visual reality of which he wrote. Artifacts we could know from museums and reconstructions but place, we thought, was different; perhaps we could situate ourselves in the poet's own angle of vision, and share the view. We were ready to see, and our readiness was both evoked and enhanced by the experience of place. We each have asked ourselves in different ways, and at different times, wherein lies the pull, where the conviction, or the fiction, of the past as real comes from, and we both have located it through, or as, place. We each have a somewhat different emphasis in our *manner* of locating, however, a difference characterized by our personalities and our theoretical outlooks. Our individual voices, both personal and scholarly, will resonate separately and distinguish themselves as our book progresses— we do see some things quite differently and on occasion disagree with each other completely—and we offer here a brief outline of our individual thinking on how we imagine our project and our purpose.

Marijane thinks in terms of "thickening" and translating; her aim in this book and in practically everything that she writes is to "thicken" (borrowing Clifford Geertz's term) the reality of the northern world of medieval literature for the reader, to make it accessible to the imaginations of those who actively enter into a world when they read a fiction. Not everyone does this or wishes to, but this book will not appeal to those who read solely academically, for ideas, thematic structures, historical fact, and the like—those who do not engage fully with the "thick" world of the text.

It is important to be as accurate as possible (within the constraints of audience and aesthetics) in translating a world as in translating a text. Such accuracy was Marijane's primary purpose when she illustrated her translation of *Beowulf* with pictures of artifacts, "treasures of the ancient north" (Osborn, 1983). But just as in the translation of a text, the translation of a world demands more than simple accuracy, or the transparency that translators once sought and believed they could achieve. It demands forms to which we can *relate,* forms, in other words, that answer our desires as we read from where and who we are. From this point of view, accuracy is only one of our desires; more important to us as engaged readers is a coherent world made accessible for us to enter. From this point of view, though both of us as readers and scholars would like to know exactly where the *Beowulf* poet was locating Beowulf's homeland, it is more important to us as readers that we have a viable homeland, a place on our mental map of the poem toward which we may turn our faces with Beowulf as he sails from Denmark. And just as in translating a crux in a text where nobody knows for certain what a phrase means, when translating a world one must sometimes take a risk, opt for what seems the most likely possibility. And to our joy, as sometimes occurs in literary translation, the possibilities we have chosen work well with the texts we were given. These northern landscapes of mainland Scandinavia and Iceland bountifully answer our readerly desire.

Gillian shares these views of the activity of translation, where text and reader are both "translated," and wants to understand how places in the texts of the past both center and decenter our readerly desires in the present. She is interested in both theorizing the experience and experiencing the theory, and in moving toward realizing some of the elusive promise of interdisciplinarity. In the course of making the journeys described in the following chapters, the idea of place became, for Gillian, catalyst and prism, a source of clarity and complexity, and a means of bringing together experience and theory. Cultural geographer Yi-Fu Tuan offers a perspective on the problems of unitary definitions of place: "An experience that good physical scientists often have, that good social scientists rarely have, and that good humanist scholars (including geographers) almost never have is the chance to jump out of their seat and shout 'Eureka!' " (1983: 70). One reason for this is that it is a function of a general question such as "what is the nature of place?" to become immediately particular, dissolving into dozens of further questions and possible directions of study that resist hierarchical evaluation.

Tuan's remarks led Gillian to examine the "Eureka impulse" and the extent to which it underlies and is embodied by the search to locate "the very place." This is perhaps especially strongly present in the Icelandic journeys, where the past landscapes of the sagas often seemed to correlate with the present geographical reality. The excitement of exactitude, of replication, is of course a variant on the search for origins, and as such it partakes of nostalgia and closure of meaning, not to mention illusion. But to suggest that medieval selves, fictional or otherwise, and modern ones have shared a point or rather a "place" of meaning is not to state that they have all fixed the "same" point, or defined the nature of this or that place. Less mysterious than any point of unified origin, and more accessible, is the idea that place is a shared form of meaning, more obviously an experience, more readily apprehended as a process rather than stasis. Medieval and modern viewpoints converge in an experience of place, an experience of others' constructions of place in conjunction with one's own, of present negotiation with the past.[3] Our experiences and images of places, whether or not they are "the very places," might then frame a kind of functional and dynamic interdisciplinarity, or a prism of semiotic convergence. They frame a newly created space where the literary, the historical, and the cultural are in ongoing negotiation with the geographical, the personal, and the material—a place to continue writing the saga.

Whether we think of ourselves as thickening, translating, or negotiating, our joint dialogue with the past is centered on place, as a theoretical possibility and as inhabited space, as a sense that individuals, whether "real" or otherwise, lived in and looked at these places that we may now live in and look at. Chiefly because of the Icelanders' continued life in the place of their saga-inscribed past, our travels in Iceland followed routes well marked in the sagas and recognizable today, whereas those we followed in *Beowulf* are heuristic rather than verifiably inscribed in the text; thus our "successes" on these two expeditions were of two different kinds, one in terms of "authentic" locations and the other in terms of workable locations. But in this book we are going further than subverting the line between authentic and workable; we are writing a professional text in which the line between permissible and impermissible forms of discourse is broken down. As Mary Louise Pratt has said, "In terms of its own metaphors, the scientific position of speech is that of an observer fixed on the edge of a space, looking in and/or down upon what is other" (1986: 32), whereas the position of the good reader (like Pratt's good ethnographer) is inside the space of the other. In this book we not only slip inside the fictional spaces of our medieval texts by relating to the people there, we also physically *go* there, hoping to take our readers too into these spaces often locked apart from experience by the scholar's and the critic's discursive practice.

As well as traveling the landscapes of the people in our texts, we people the landscapes we have traveled, and we invest them with our own desires. To various degrees, the following accounts take note of our own critical activity, and we conclude with a more self-conscious examination of our desire for the landscape in an attempt to recount the saga we created of the saga that we traced. Our chapters will aim to make further connections in addition to those prompted by the interaction and intersection of our own desires in and for the landscape. These landscapes can connect the outer world that we all share with the more private world of response to the told story. They connect the literal with the literary, the present with the past, the private domain with the public.

We are not attempting to prove anything about the texts themselves, as Schliemann was endeavoring in his desire-driven and less than candidly reported excavations of "Troy" (see Traill, 1984), and as Thor Heyerdahl and Tim Severin were doing on their reenactments of heroic voyages. Rather, as we traverse these spaces and places we hope to open up a new and essentially interdisciplinary space, one that facilitates a conversation among disciplinary viewpoints, and between the personal and professional. As we use a variety of approaches and borrow from different disciplines, we also employ an array of styles. Endnotes appear together with journal entries, travelogue with dialogue, anecdotes with analysis, and theoretical speculation along with the narrative of personal practice. Moreover, we repeat ourselves and we often revise. We offer our repetitions as expansions, similar points being made usually for different reasons.

Our revisions have most often been a function of the experience of travel. We start with one plan and adopt another—sometimes literally in midstream—and this process continually reveals the existence of our own preconceived "mind maps." We obtained our first ideas about mental maps from Jonathan Wylie and David Margolin's book about the Faroe Islands, *The Ring of Dancers,* in which they discuss both images and idioms of orientation, including conceptual maps. Conceptual maps usually offer the point of view of someone who dwells in a place and projects his or her idea of this home place as opposed to other places. The European-centered map of the world is an obvious example. The New Yorker's map of the United States in which New York City extends over most of the map is a parody of this mode that situates the mapmaking culture at the center. It is a joke with a bite, however, because many New Yorkers would feel, whether or not they would be willing to admit it, that there was a subjective accuracy about the way the relationship between the City and Outside-the-City was represented here. As opposed to the map of the world that purports to be a realistic representation of geography, the "Big Apple" map takes liberties with external reality to project a more human reality. Direction and naming similarly reveal this self-reflecting view of the landscape. At Oxford University, when a student is thrown out or expelled (the usual term elsewhere), he or she is "sent down" in Oxford terms. One might think this expression represents a map orientation that places Oxford north (up) from London. Yet when even a Scot may be "sent down," the university becomes situated on a pinnacle in relationship to all the rest of creation. This is not an

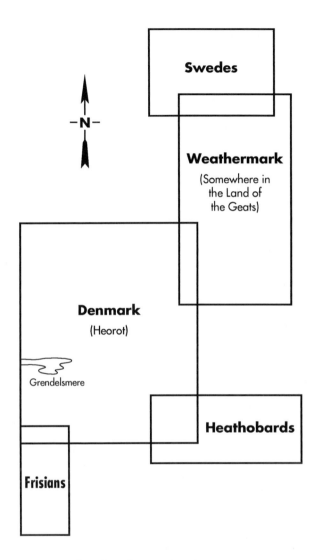

Figure 1. The tribes of *Beowulf*. Preliminary conceptual map, 1984.

inaccurate representation of a feeling actually found in Oxford. The etymology of many names that native populations use to describe themselves similarly indicates that "we" are the normal ones, human beings, the "people," whereas others, foreigners, are in some sense subnormal—naturally enough, because they live outside, down there, elsewhere.

Nearly a decade ago, the idea of conceptual maps in *The Ring of Dancers* inspired our drawing of *Beowulf* maps of Scandinavia (figure 1).

At first we tried to keep any idea of the real Scandinavia vague, which was not too difficult given that our knowledge of Scandinavian geography *was* vague. Near the map's center, of course, was Heorot (the Danish hall of the hart, the heart), probably accurately enough placed in terms both of the poem and of the poet. The land of the Danes was big. Somewhere "down there" toward modern Paris was where Hygelac raided and lost his life.[4] To the southwest lay Finnsburg, that place in Frisia where Hengest fought King Finn, perhaps imagined by the poet as afterward leading his retainers in a direct line onward to southern Britain. The major problem and the point of the exercise was the "land of the Geats" (we will use this anglicization of the name throughout): where did the poem offer a sense that Beowulf's homeland lay? Because of the frequent skirmishes with the Sweon (Swedes) mentioned in the second half of the poem, it seemed to us that Beowulf's people lived over in that direction, somewhere between Heorot and Uppsala, and our first conceptual map represents this orientation by placing the Geats in southwest Sweden (setting aside for the time being the problem of the "sea" between these peoples). This location is not simply based on the text, however; it is influenced by the early-twentieth-century nationalistic quarrels between Danish and Swedish scholars, the Danes wanting to claim Beowulf and his Geats as Jutes, the Swedes (probably more accurately) believing the Geats were the Gautar. Thus before we ever thought of going to Scandinavia, the act of drawing the map began to engage us, to make us aware of the problems and desirous to find out "the truth." We were first driven to the atlas; then, when opportunity arose, to the physical places themselves.

How much does being there change one's orientation to place? When we began to draw a second series of mind maps during the writing of this introduction, in order to get an idea of how both reading maps and going there had affected our sense of direction, we found that while certain elements remained constant, others had shifted. We also found that visiting a place possibly connected with the story definitely tips the balance in its favor, as confirmation of its reality as place makes it seem more likely to be "the very place" than any place not visited. Therefore on our personal mental maps Beowulf's land is precisely located now in a place we know. Located much farther north than it was before, and changing the Geatish-Swedish orientation, it is also smaller than before. But we had trouble drawing a map, because we realized that the land of Beowulf's Geats was a land without boundaries. Nor could we draw the land of the Danes; for Gillian it was a patch two miles square around Heorot itself, but for

Marijane it covered all of southern Scandinavia. Thus the map shifts and changes as we project upon it our experience and our understanding.

Yi-Fu Tuan sees perception of place, in fact the very content of what is observed, as a massive and complex synthesis of cultural, experiential, and environmental attitudes, conditioned by a myriad of factors such as gender, age, and class, among many others. A landscape, writes Tuan, is "a construct of the mind and of feeling" (1979: 89); "it is not a given, a piece of reality that is simply there" (100), but an effort of the imagination, an "ordering of reality from different angles" (90), a combining in the mind's eye of elements both objective and subjective. The terrain of place is then substantially internal, the picture made within the frame of individual perception. Tuan requires that we consider our own role in the creation of landscape, a process that both complicates and enriches any understanding of places of the past, as they are perceived in the present.

Even though we are thus conscious of ourselves in the places we visit and of our observing them through all our subjectivities, and we use theoretical devices such as mind maps and the plethora of theoretical tools that are available to us today, the idea of actually traveling to the place of the event (whether fictional or "real"), or of mixing personal and scholarly narratives, is certainly not new. As our project is grounded in and gains impetus from new critical developments in medieval studies (see note 2), it also reflects a long-established mode of inquiry. The enterprises of the ethnographer or the travel writer have a long and varied history, as Pratt well describes. Within our own discipline, several *Beowulf* scholars of the nineteenth century sought to stand, or at least to imagine that they could stand, in "the very place" the poet had in mind. In our saga journeys that are related in chapters 2 and 3 we were very specifically following in W. G. Collingwood's 1897 footsteps and relying on his watercolor sketches of "sagasteads." Indeed, our enterprise repeats in some respects a "tropology of travel writing" (Pratt, 1986: 42), insofar as we include in this introduction some description of the personal rationale of our project. But we want to avoid relegating this information to the margins of our text, where Pratt suggests that it often remains (31–32), or to claim that what follows is that ethnographic "wild goose" known as "neutral, tropeless discourse" (27).

It also bears emphasizing that what we were doing was not an unusual activity for women. Our path in Sweden overlapped that of Mary Wollstonecraft on her information-gathering tour of 1795, and later in the nineteenth century many of the travelers seeking literary or historical goals were women, often traveling in pairs. Our enterprise may even be in the tradition of medieval travel literature; one thinks at once of

Egeria and of the well-traveled Wife of Bath, indeed of the Canterbury pilgrimage itself. Mary B. Campbell discovers many instances of collaboration and reinterpretation throughout the accounts of medieval travelers, noting that the genre characteristically abounds in forms of mediation (Campbell, 1988: 34). Travelers tell stories, to others and to each other, and they regularly edit, expand, and invent.

This book tells our own stories of travel, and in it we talk to each other as well as to the reader. We both contribute individual sections to each of the three chapters, and we move from Beowulf country on the mainland to saga places in Iceland. The chapters follow the actual chronology of our journeys and chart our progress, insofar as they show our increasing theoretical awareness, and, in Gillian's case, the development of photographic skills from poor (which is why there are no photos by Gillian in the first chapter) to the capacity to create a reproducible image. Gillian took all photos for this book, with the exception of plate 1, taken by Randolph Swearer, and plate 14, taken by Marijane. Also, with a view to producing a more readable text, we have normalized many Scandinavian spellings, usually following the translations we have used.

The first chapter contains the accounts of two "Beowulf" journeys, one by sea in 1985 and the other by land in 1988; the latter contains Marijane's justification for locating Beowulf's Swedish homeland where she does, composed in a more traditional scholarly mode but with glances over her shoulder at herself doing the locating. In chapter 2 we move more radically into theory, addressing matters both Beowulfian and Icelandic, as well as what it might mean to "desire" a landscape in these post-Lacanian days. In chapter 3 we each tell our own story of "the road to Drangey," the volcanic island where Grettir the Outlaw held out for his last two winters—how we finally succeeded in getting there and what we found when we did. We offer these two accounts of our shared experience instead of a formal conclusion, with the conviction that the dialogue and difference that they represent in turn best represents the overarching premises of our project.

In the spirit of journeys taken, then, and in various modes yet always our own voices, we offer these stories of places.

CHAPTER 1

Mapping *Beowulf*

Reinventing Beowulf's Voyage to Denmark

The academic approach to these matters is admirably illustrated in certain characteristic pronouncements of the late Professor E. G. R. Taylor, who, regardless of the fact that at no time in her career was she capable of getting a rowing-boat across the Round Pond, would not hesitate to pass judgement on the professional competence of some of the greatest mariners in history.

G. J. Marcus, The Conquest of the North Atlantic

In August 1985 we attempted to "reinvent" Beowulf's voyage to Heorot. Marijane will give some of the scholarly reasons for our journey in the next section of this chapter; what follows first is an account of the voyage, the experience of it, what we had hoped to discover and what we actually learned. This is a tale—some might call it a tall one—told as a story, rather than a history, of a sea journey. It is necessarily a partial story, for all those reasons that we discussed in the Introduction, and also an experiment in that it mixes more formal scholarly and informal personal narrative styles. I had originally written this account for scholarly publication (Overing, 1988), and had revised and pruned it repeatedly to eradicate anything that smacked of the personal or the anecdotal. In doing so I watched a vital part of the process of "reinvention" reduced to the facts that did not fully describe the experience, and I take pleasure now in reinstating those elements of the story that were considered inappropriate before. I shall move from "I" to "we" and include reflections from my own journal as well as anecdotal information, navigational facts, and academic references.

One other point should be made clear from the outset: we do not offer our experience as a replica of an actual voyage undertaken by a real person. We do not claim the scientific authority of the kind of expeditions led by Thor Heyerdahl—despite the fact that Marijane has been recently designated the "Thor Heyerdahl of Old English studies" (Liuzza, 1991:

34). We emphasize instead the more speculative, imaginative, and fictional enterprise suggested by the term "reinvention"; our twofold aim was to recover some sense of what seafaring might have been like in the time of the poet, and to locate the poem in our imagination and in that of our students—placing its actions on our mental maps. Neither of us was an expert sailor, but we had a great deal of enthusiasm, the aid of an excellent crew, a sturdy boat, institutional funding (which we gratefully acknowledge), and a lot of luck. Like so many of the journeys we have taken, this one represented in special measure a coming together in place and time of a number of disparate and apparently random factors. And curiously, we learned more about the world of the poem in those days at sea than many hours of teaching and studying could reveal to us. In addition to its historical and geographic interest, the voyage turned out to be a reimagining of our own conception of the people and places, of the poetry of *Beowulf*; it enabled us to act out and through the conceptual maps that we brought to the enterprise.

Studies have demonstrated that the *Beowulf* poet had a sound sense of the history and material culture of the period of his poem. Marijane has illustrated this finding by placing photographs of real artifacts alongside references to identical or similar items in the text of *Beowulf* in her translation of the poem (Osborn, 1983). Just as we thought that the poet had a clearer and more accurate idea than formerly believed of the concrete, or nonimaginary, things he was talking about, we wished also to challenge persistent doubts, at one time voiced by Klaeber, as to whether he had any "clear knowledge of Northern geography" (1950: xlvii). Unlike Huppé, who follows Leake in claiming that the Geats are among the imaginary elements of the poem, inhabiting "a legendary land placed somewhere in Scandinavia" (1984: 13–14), we believed with many Scandinavian historians and most recently R. T. Farrell that the Geats were the historical Gautar. This tribe inhabited southern Sweden before being assimilated by the Svear, the tribe (called the Sweon in *Beowulf*) from which modern Sweden gets its name.[1] But where among the Geats were Beowulf's people located, where was the Wedermark from which he sailed? We know where he goes: he sails to Heorot, placed by most scholars at Gammel Lejre, the ancient seat of the Scylding kings near Roskilde (though some would place it at Roskilde itself).[2]

We also "know" that the journey took Beowulf one to two days, if we are to believe the poet's reference to his arrival "on the next day" ("oþres dogores"; *Beowulf*, 219).[3] This raises some further questions. How was a day measured by the *Beowulf* poet? G. J. Marcus suggests some factors for consideration:

In the sagas and various other sources, the distances between a number of points in the North Atlantic are reckoned in terms of "day's sailing," *dœgr-sigling*. A word of explanation is required here. Strictly speaking, the term *dœgr* (day) meant a period of twelve hours, since, according to the *Rímbegla*, an astronomical and geodetic treatise compiled in Iceland in the late thirteenth century, in a day there were two *dœgra* and in a *dœgr* there were twelve hours. But in point of fact, *dœgr-sigling* sometimes covered twelve, and sometimes twenty-four, hours. The matter is indeed a highly complex one, abounding in inconsistencies. (1980: 109)

Did these kinds of distinctions matter to the *Beowulf* poet, or did they have any currency during the Old English period? In "The Voyages of Ohthere and Wulfstan," sailing time is recorded in terms of the period of daylight; Wulfstan specifies that when the occasion arises he has to sail by both day *and* night (Lund, 1984: 22). But he, like us, was a primarily coastal sailor and made camp at night when coastal landmarks could not be sighted. The time of year would, of course, make a great deal of difference in the length of daylight. I raise these questions here not to answer them, but to show that even in a matter as apparently simple as defining a day, we are still on conjectural ground, and our project of reinvention is seen as just that. (We decided to use Crumlin-Pedersen's hypothetical sailing times as our best gauge, as I shall explain.)

Our next challenge was to discover a suitable departure point. On the assumption that the Göta Älv, the river served by the modern port city of Göteborg, was linked with the tribal name of the Gautar or Geats (first suggested to Marijane by C. L. Wrenn), we took that port as our departure point, hoping to complete the voyage within the two days reported in the poem, and also hoping that the land formations mentioned there might be discovered along the way (despite their apparently formulaic quality). Our goal was to examine the suggestion of Klaeber and others that the poet was using geography indiscriminately. Instead, we thought, we might be able to show that he had some sense of the geographical relationships of the northern tribes he mentions. Another good reason to undertake such a project was the fact that no one else had done so. For my own part, I was inclined to take seriously Marcus's complaints about "armchair" scholars of maritime history—though I strongly suspect that his comment on Professor Taylor's rowing ability, quoted in the epigraph to this section, might be overly harsh.

Our initial rationale for the voyage was both clarified and modified by the actual experience at sea, demonstrating well that "as to what is and what is not possible at sea, the mariner must necessarily be the ultimate authority" (Marcus, 1980: xii). We had planned to use Ohthere's account of his second voyage from Sciringesheal to Hedeby as a guide; the route he describes partially overlapped ours, and his documentary, eyewitness account of seafaring conditions and distances (one of the staples of beginning Old English courses) provided us with coordinates. Despite considerable research on the historical voyages of Ohthere and Wulfstan, and a recent book edited by Niels Lund, *Two Voyagers at the Court of King Alfred*, no one has undertaken an actual reenactive voyage. In his contribution to *Two Voyagers*, an essay entitled "Ships, Navigation and Routes in the Reports of Ohthere and Wulfstan," Ole Crumlin-Pedersen, the director of the Viking Ship Museum at Roskilde, maps out possible routes, and calculates sailing times and distances based on analyses of sailing techniques in the Viking period and of the maritime characteristics of the area. We hoped to take practical advantage of the careful research of Crumlin-Pedersen and other scholars included in *Two Voyagers*, as well as contributing some information of our own about Beowulf's imaginary voyage.

Our boat was a forty-two-foot yacht, the *Galadriel*. Although I had observed briefly in my journal that it was "beautiful, large, elegant," in fact at first sight it was quite breathtaking, especially to a novice sailor like myself: handmade and hand-finished, sleek with polished woods and sweeping angles, compact and built for speed. Peter Bolwig, its captain and owner, had spent three years building it, crafting every plank and door handle. Our crew consisted of Peter (boatbuilder, classic-car restorer, professional captain, and grower of organic vegetables) and a first mate, Kristian Fabricius (schoolteacher, folklore historian, weekend sailor, and Peter's longtime friend). Marijane and I would learn and assist as we could. We began the ten-day voyage from Kørsør, a harbor on the west coast of the island of Zealand in Denmark, where the *Galadriel* was berthed. We sailed three days with fair winds from there to our projected point of departure, Göteborg, sailing through one night and stopping for the second on the small Danish island of Anholt (see figure 2).

[16 August. Continued sailing through the night, occasionally getting up to 6–7 knots. Midday. We can see the island of Anholt. Famous for its beautiful beaches. More wind now, after coming to an almost standstill pre-dawn. This is called the dogwatch, Peter informed me, the worst time to be on deck, especially when nothing is happening or moving, neither wind nor sky. Correspondence

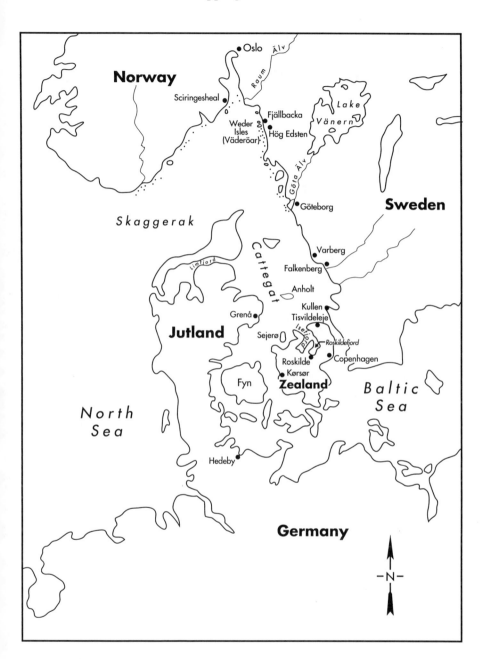

Figure 2. Map of the Cattegat.

with the uht—*the hour when the exile bewails his care in* The
Wanderer*? We have come seventy-five miles in twenty-three
hours, not bad, not good, according to the crew. Very good time
considering the low winds. Cliffs and beaches of Anholt clearly
visible now.* Of course *there are "shining headlands" in Denmark.
I am looking at one now that requires only the appearance of sunlight to qualify.]*

Although our reinvention of the voyage proper did not commence
until we reached Sweden, a movement of the imagination had already
begun. Leaving the coast at Kørsør and approaching Anholt, we realized
that the Danish landscape was not so flat as some *Beowulf* commentators, arguing that the poet's landscape has little to do with reality, have
suggested. There were cliffs, indeed "sea-cliffs shining" ("brimclifu bli-
can"; *Beowulf*, 222). For my own part (as an Englishwoman), I was developing a sense of what this land and sea looked like independent of my
own, hitherto unacknowledged, associations. The world of the poem was
starting to look different to me, assuming a vital and distinct visual
reality.

*[17 August. Left Anholt at 6 A.M. for Göteborg. Weather bad,
steady rain and little wind. We are making 4 knots, using the
engine, waiting for a wind. The notion of waiting/hoping for
weather comes alive. Ohthere refers twice to waiting for a wind.
Steely gray sky and sea. Marijane made a point about the
"Scandinavianness" of* Beowulf—*what this land and sea* look *like
is important in our total conception of the poem. These aren't the
cliffs of Dover or the Channel, but they have a similar feel.]*

Somewhere between leaving Anholt and arriving in Göteborg, our
plans changed. After a day of slow wind and constant rain spent inside
the cabin, consulting maps and sources and questioning the crew, Marijane began to be persuaded that the *Wedermearc*, the starting point for
Beowulf's voyage, had to be located in what is now Bohuslän, the coastal
area extending north of modern Göteborg to near Oslo Fjord. During that
long, wet day at sea, she convinced the crew and myself that the northern
part of the Cattegat coast of Sweden was the best imaginative and geographically realistic location for Beowulf's interactions with other tribes
and for his heroic exploits. Indeed, our crew did not require much convincing and took up our emended course with enthusiasm, Kristian being
particularly interested by the evidence of local antiquities that Marijane
had amassed.

Perhaps what drew us most compellingly in the direction of Bohuslän was treasure. The treasure-burial site at Hög Edsten, close to Fjällbacka (a small town in the Väderö Fjord area), has been dated 500–550 A.D., approximately the right date to correspond with events in the poem. During the excavation of this mound in 1863, a sword hilt was discovered that was almost identical to that found later at Sutton Hoo. Also, the greatest concentration of Bronze Age rock carvings is found in this area. Bohuslän province is the richest in carvings in Sweden, with eleven hundred to twelve hundred engraved rock faces, four hundred of which are at Tanum, a site close to Fjällbacka. Ships and boats are among the most common type of carving, attesting to an ancient tradition of seafaring in the Väderöfjord area.

As we approached the entrance to Göteborg harbor, another indicative piece of information came into perspective. Even in our twentieth-century craft, we had to navigate our way through the outlying, treacherous skerries using landmarks as a guide. There were many landmarks of various shapes and sizes, some with histories and names (like the well-known "Sven Edvin" lighthouse that guards the entrance to Göteborg harbor). These are still indispensable to both day and night navigation; the navigator depends on their distinctive shapes by day and on their lights by night. Beowulf's last wish to have a mound built on a promontory as a landmark for seafarers seems to show the poet's understanding of the navigational needs of the day. A well-placed landmark would be as fine and useful a legacy to a seafaring people as treasure.

[17 August. Rain all day and no wind, arrived Göteborg soaked at about 8 P.M. Ate dinner in an Italian restaurant. The Swedes look so young. A country of real contradictions. A "sobering board" of social workers against alcoholism, folkhög schools where you can learn what you want, and lots of people drinking, drinking.]

After docking in Göteborg, the next day we drove the additional sixty miles up the coast to Fjällbacka, as our schedule did not permit us sailing time for this segment of our journey. The single most striking aspect of this resort town is the enormous land formation overlooking the harbor, a landmark visible for miles from the many outlying islands (see plate 1), two of which are named the Väderöar (Marijane elaborates on the importance of *väder* as a place-name element in the next section). As Beowulf sets off on his expedition to Denmark, his boat awaits him "under" (i.e., "at the foot" of) a mountain ("bat under beorge"; *Beowulf,* 211). The harbor of Fjällbacka in Väderöfjord would have been an ideal *beorg* for

Beowulf to set out from. After an examination of the treasure site and rock carvings, we returned to Göteborg, excited at the possibility that we might be in "Beowulf country."

[18 August. Left Göteborg by car, went north seventy-five kilo-meters to Fjällbacka, nearest town to Hög Edsten ("high oath-stone"). Site of treasure burial, 500–550 A.D., sword found like that at Sutton Hoo. Are we near the burial place of Beowulf? Fjällbacka is a lovely harbor town; we arrived late in the season, town quiet, sunny day. The town is completely dominated by the presence of this vast rock shape. We shall attempt to find the oath-stone . . . We didn't—or rather we looked at several undistin-guished mounds (Iron Age). Picnicked by one of many dazzling lakes, after looking at Bronze Age carvings. On to Lake Vänern, enormous, calm, fairy-tale-like reflections in water. We agreed that it was like something out of Tolkien . . .]

Were we inventing a sense of place, conjuring a spirit of place, discovering our selves in place? I later recalled Yi-Fu Tuan's remarks in his essay on "Geopiety": "In ancient Greece, tombs of heroes and sanctuaries were common features in the landscape . . . Heroes protected the soil and stood ready to help their fellow countrymen in all their needs. The bones and ashes of heroes continued to exert this power. Heroes thus provided a link between the past and the present" (1976: 21).

We regretted that we were unable to take the time to sail to Fjällbacka and begin the voyage from there. Peter and Kristian had sailed from Göteborg to Fjällbacka on several occasions, and, after consulting them about sailing times and conditions, we were satisfied that our departure from the southern end of the province of Bohuslän would be approximately compensated for by the time taken to complete the laborious and slow exit from Göteborg harbor, down the Göta Älv and into the open sea of the Cattegat.

On the first day of our voyage proper, we left Göteborg around 8 A.M. in heavy rain and a light wind. The rain persisted most of the day, but the wind improved so that we could average 6–7 knots, covering about sixty-five nautical miles and arriving in Falkenberg by 8:30 P.M. Falkenberg is about five miles farther down the Swedish coast than Galtaback (south of modern Varberg), where Crumlin-Pedersen proposes that Ohthere might have put into harbor on the second day of his voyage from Sciringesheal to Hedeby. (Ohthere had probably set out that day from Orust, just south of the Väderöar area, where there would have been many good overnight anchorages.) Ohthere's five-day voyage of 375 miles would have required an average daily rate of about eighty miles, an average speed of 5 knots, and a sailing time of sixteen hours each day. Such progress also assumes steady winds and good luck. An element of pride or boasting about such luck may appear in Ohthere's account; Crumlin-Pedersen states that he reported "his best sailing times, rather as modern yachtsmen would prefer to talk about their fastest passages than those on which they were forced to lie waiting for a favourable wind" (1984: 30).[4]

On the second day ("oþres dogores"; *Beowulf*, 219) we had to decide between two possible routes. Following Ohthere's course, we would sail down the Swedish coast to the promontory of Kullen, where it is possible to see the northern tip of Zealand (see figure 2). This would have been the obvious turning point for Ohthere, a landmark sailor who possessed no compass, to cross over to Denmark. But the chances of completing our journey to Roskilde by the end of the second day—in the amount of time it took Beowulf—were slim if we took this route. The quicker way would be to take a diagonal across open sea. We asked our captain and first mate to put themselves in Beowulf's position: if you were a landmark, coastal sailor, with a good general knowledge of seafaring (your father Ecgtheow has traveled this route before) and an inclination to take chances (witness the contest with Breca), would you cross this stretch of open sea with no compass? As experienced sailors of the Cattegat, they both assured us that this was entirely possible and not overly dangerous, because in this area one would never be more than a few hours from land in any direction. The only real variable, or possible hazard, would be the same for modern sailors as it must have been for Beowulf: the weather, and the extent of visibility.

[20 August. Question: How could Beowulf have crossed a diagonal of open sea with no compass? Peter says that if you and your family had a good general knowledge of the seas and of which land was where, then "of course you could make it." All you might do is end up in Jutland, perhaps. After all, Hans Henryk (a friend of Peter) in his "foolhardy youth" went from Zealand-Odd (northwest point of Zealand) to Grenå (east coast of Jutland), out of sight of land, and in a twenty-two-foot sailboat. Peter likes this story . . . Kristian says, "I would definitely do it. I would hit Zealand at some point. There are no holes . . . " (Note: There are "holes"—the two "belts" of water on each side of Zealand; what Kristian meant was, once passing below the top of that island one is never out of sight of land.) Kristian's grandfather used to sail up the very narrow and dangerous Limfjord at night or in fog simply

by smelling his way along! Kristian says it's even better to sail
open sea at night, stars are clearer.]

Our crew's easy acceptance—indeed, dismissal of—this challenge of crossing open sea accords well with recent research on the range and scope of Viking seafaring ability. To the frequently posed question of "How were the Norsemen able, with such apparent confidence and certainty, to cross and re-cross enormous stretches of open sea, at a time when not merely the quadrant and astrolabe, but even the magnetic compass, were as yet unknown?" (Marcus, 1980: 106), Marcus replies with a wide range of evidence. Norse sailors were able to make use of a great variety of adventitious aids to navigation, such as the flight patterns of birds, coastal landmarks, the color and temperature of the water, and the movement of plankton, whales, and ice floes; coastal pilots were highly skilled, and some, like our first mate's grandfather, "had such an intimate knowledge of their own particular stretch of coast that they were able after nightfall to steer a vessel up the long Norwegian fjords by the light of the stars" (116). Norse mariners used "dead reckoning" (estimating a ship's position by means of courses steered and distance covered), latitude sailing, and calculation according to the position of heavenly bodies (100–18). Not only do we find the term *hafvilla* in Old Norse, which denotes a state of no reckoning and complete loss of direction at sea, but Marcus also shows how the language "covers every phase of life afloat" (106).

It may be dangerous to conflate evidence of ninth- and tenth-century Norse voyages with the mythohistorical sailing expertise of the earlier Geats, and with the poet's reinvention of it, but we can assume with some confidence a shared seafaring tradition and a body of knowledge that developed by means of oral transmission and personal experience. Marcus emphasizes the oral nature of navigational knowledge in many instances; notably, he records that the "directions" to Greenland were not written down until the fourteenth century, when this thousand-mile voyage had been regularly made for several hundred years (95).

In the light of such impressive expertise, our short crossing to Denmark seemed a simple matter. Further assured by our crew's conviction and enthusiasm, we left Falkenberg at 6 A.M. and took the diagonal course across open sea in the hope of completing our journey in two days. Around midafternoon, as we approached Tisvildeleje, we began to see our first glimpses of the Danish coastline. As we sailed closer to Zealand, the coastline became increasingly clearer and more impressive in the bright afternoon sunlight. Whether by coincidence or not, as we approached the coast of Zealand and sailed around to Isefjord, which leads to Roskilde, we saw landmarks in precisely the order of the poem:

> . . . ða liðende   land gesawon,
> brimclifu blican   beorgas steape
> side sænæssas.

> . . . the seafarers saw land, sea-cliffs shining,
> steep hills, broad promontories.
>
> (*Beowulf*, 221–23)

These landmarks appear in just this order so spectacularly that one wonders whether the poet did not know something about this approach, either personally or by hearsay.[5] (At this point I most acutely regretted my poor photographic skills and lack of a telephoto lens.) In a conversation the following day in his office at the Viking Ship Museum, Ole Crumlin-Pedersen commented that because seafarers of those days had neither writing nor instruments, perhaps they used verbal sea charts for approaches to landfalls as important as this one. Marijane has since followed up this suggestion and discovered some interesting parallels, which she presents in the fifth section of chapter 2. In fact, the idea of an "oral map" is borne out in several ways. In his overall assessment of Norse seamanship, Marcus repeatedly emphasizes the oral transmission of traditional navigational knowledge. When Bjarni Herjolfsson sailed from Iceland to join his father in Greenland, for example, he must have had a very clear sense of what he was looking for, and of how to find it. Although he was driven off course three times, and faced an increasingly mutinous crew, he refused to explore any of these unknown shores (bypassing North America in the process). Their appearance simply did not accord with the descriptions of the Greenland coastline that he had been given. His sailing expertise rescued him from several states of *hafvilla*, and he did find his way to the right coastline: " 'This tallies most closely with what I have been told about Greenland,' replied Bjarni. 'And here we shall go in to land' " (*Grænlendinga Saga*, 54).

[*20 August. Tuesday. 4:30 P.M. Sunny, great wind. Sailing past Hundested and pressing on to Roskilde. If Beowulf had wind like this, he surely made it in two days. We should make it by 8:00 or so. Would not have believed it this morning.*]

Later the same afternoon, as we sailed past Hundested into Isefjord, the wind picked up considerably and our speed increased from an average of 5–6 knots to 8 knots. We began to believe that we might indeed complete our journey in two days. As we had only a 30 percent chance of getting such a good wind in this area at any time of the year, we felt extremely lucky; like Ohthere and Beowulf, we too had an easy crossing of the "wave-paths" (*Beowulf*, 228).

We sailed down to Roskilde, completing a total of eighty-three miles, and arrived at approximately 8:30 P.M.; we waited until the next day to make the six-mile journey overland to Gammel Lejre (where Klaeber places Heorot). The final stage of our journey from Isefjord down through Roskilde Fjord to the harbor of Roskilde was not without mishap. First we encountered a yacht race, with flocks of yachts sailing against us. Then the waters of the upper part of Roskilde Fjord—a true "swan-road" (*Beowulf*, 200), with a traffic of actual swans—proved extremely difficult to navigate, and would have been equally difficult for Beowulf and his men. The water level in Roskilde Fjord has not changed a great deal since the Viking period, probably fluctuating no more than a half meter above or below its present level. The fjord is so shallow (two meters in places) that on one occasion when we passed a broken buoy on the wrong side by about two or three meters, we promptly ran aground. Though our six-foot keel would have reached deeper than that of the ship Beowulf might have navigated, getting to Roskilde by way of Roskilde Fjord would have been problematic for the Geats. Crumlin-Pedersen suggests that Beowulf might have had a land-based warning system, as former local pilots' stopovers are indicated by place-names in the fjord. He might have picked up a pilot at Kulhuse or Lynaes, two harbors further up Roskilde Fjord, to guide him down to a disembarkation point near the foot of the fjord (today's Roskilde). He could then have marched or ridden the eighteen to twenty miles to Heorot (Gammel Lejre). This would accord with the poem, where the mounted Danish coast guard leads Beowulf and his men along the road to Hrothgar's hall.

One other outside possibility would be that Beowulf approached Heorot by sailing inland up the Lejre River. When we saw this river, it looked rather like a large creek, but the channel indicates that it was once far larger; it has been diminished by a local pumping station. One thousand years ago, again according to our conversation with Crumlin-Pedersen, the river could easily have accommodated a small vessel.

We completed the journey to Gammel Lejre by taxi, however, and explored a neighboring outdoor museum that appeared to me to be a species of Iron Age Colonial Williamsburg—a replica of daily living conditions of the period, complete with fearsome-looking livestock and low-lying cramped dwellings that were a far cry from the towering gabled image of Heorot. The hollowed-out horse carcasses displayed in the sacrificial bog were sufficiently unnerving, though this was also the site of human sacrifice if we are to believe Thietmar of Merseberg's eleventh-century account (Karras, 1988: 71). We were content to explore the site of Heorot and its environs—and refrained from mounting a search for Grendel's mere . . .

[22 August. Left Roskilde at 10 A.M. for Sejerø. Very rough sailing. High winds and waves. Got into Sejerø at 10:30 P.M. after a very scary patch. Peter up on deck in dark trying to get sails down in the squall. Ran aground on rock one hundred yards from the harbor.

23 August. Same again. Left Sejerø at 8:30, very rough weather. I was sick and in my cabin most of the time.]

During the return journey from Roskilde to Kørsør we experienced our worst weather conditions. The steady battering we received from rain and unusually high winds and waves—and the repeated small-craft warnings that came over the radio as we raced for harbor—reinforced our sense that in our voyage from Sweden we had indeed been extremely lucky, and that such good luck had brought us into accord with the poem. The lines describing the voyage in *Beowulf* (210–28) are among the most dynamic and exciting in the poem, conveying a sense of speed, enthusiasm, and general good fortune. We were aware that this same passage had been much examined, even being used to support conflicting theories about the way the poem was composed (for example, oral formulaic theories of origin and the theory of classical borrowing; see note 5). We felt, however, that in "reinventing" the voyage, whether or not our location was precisely "right," we had affirmed yet another possible aspect of these lines—the poet's practical understanding of what he was talking about.

Our experience at sea gave us a clearer visual sense of the world of the poem and helped us to imagine some of the possible conditions of seafaring in the time of the *Beowulf* poet. We believe that teachers and students of the poem can benefit greatly from such a direct and realistic attention to the text. By this we do not mean that all should sail the Cattegat—though it is an experience we can recommend—but at least that there is great value in conceiving of Beowulf's voyage, and voyages like his, as taking place in the nonfictional world. Such a world has salt spray in the air, the hum of straining ropes and the flapping of sail, and a route that may actually be traversed. Not only does such imagining bring the world of *Beowulf* into sharper focus, but it also allows that familiar staple of Old English courses, "The Voyages of Ohthere and Wulfstan," a share in the excitement of adventure on real seas.

Traveling Home with Beowulf

"All the great narratives of world literature contain maps," claims Claude Gandelman, "maps that we can read" (1991: 81). If one does not find it necessary to link this claim to intentionality, it may be true. We have found it true of *Beowulf*.

Even though the poem is English, Beowulf's great deeds take place in Scandinavia: first on the island Zealand in Denmark, where he kills the fiendish monster Grendel and his avenging mother when they have attacked the hall of the Scylding king, and then in his own homeland *Wedermearc* (line 298), henceforth modernized to Wedermark, where he slays a fifty-foot-long firedragon.[6] According to traditions recounted by Snorri Sturluson and others, the dynastic home of the historical Scylding Danes is at Lejre, but no one really knows where Beowulf's homeland is. As Gillian has remarked, most scholars place it vaguely across from Zealand in the large southern Swedish province of Västergötland, "Land of the West Götar"—of the once-independent medieval Gautar who inhabited all of southern Sweden—because the poet calls Beowulf's tribe by the cognate name Geatas. (He also calls them Wedergeatas and Wederas; I shall refer to them with all three names.) Other scholars have located Beowulf's homeland in Danish Jutland or the Baltic islands Öland and Gotland off the east coast of Sweden.[7] The sailing time given in the poem, two days at most (line 219), makes these distant islands impossible, and I am going to rule out Jutland more arbitrarily (putting the Jute argument in notes), as both the etymology of the name Geatas and place-names to be discussed later suggest the Swedish mainland.

At a recent Berkeley conference titled "Understanding *Beowulf*" (April 1993), a lively exchange occurred between Professors John Niles, Theodore Andersson, and John Lindow concerning the map labeled "The Geography of *Beowulf*" in Klaeber's edition of the poem (viii). Professor Niles had delivered a paper arguing that *Beowulf* was a myth put together by an English poet for a political purpose, a view I find attractive. But he seemed to feel it important to his argument to demote Beowulf's Geats to a mythical tribe. He demonstrated how this tribe did not fit the story's geography by showing us Klaeber's map, with, as Klaeber calls them, the Geatas (alias Gautar) in the south of Sweden and the Sweon

due north. Niles pointed out, as have others before him, that in this location the Geats would not have found it necessary in their wars against
the Swedes to cross *ofer sæ*, "over the sea," as the poem says (lines 2380
and 2394). In reply, both Scandinavianists argued for the identity of the
Geats with the Gautar. Professor Andersson suggested that huge Lake
Vänern was the "sea" to be crossed, and various members of the audience
agreed that cognates of the word "sea" could mean "lake" in the various
Germanic languages. Professor Lindow nevertheless agreed with Professor Niles that Klaeber's map was wrong ("a terrible map," he said),
because it offers a misleading location for the Sweon (Svear or Swedes).
Their dynastic home was not in the central highlands of Sweden as the
map implies, but rather on the east coast around Uppsala, not far from
modern Stockholm. This true location, Lindow felt, further complicated
the problem of the Geats' crossing of water, but he did not want to elim-
inate them for this reason.

I do not find the historicity of the Geats a problem either for Niles's
argument or my own. Only the map presents a problem, and with it Klaeber's north-south orientation of these two major tribes so that the southern Geats have "trouble from their northern foes" (xl). If Beowulf's Geats
did exist, it seems unlikely that they were "the" Gautar, as such, of
southern Sweden. Only in *Beowulf* do the Geats or Gautar have the alternative name Wederas (or Weder-Geats), and I believe this name is significant, as is the problem of the "sea" they crossed, which I will discuss.
Whether they were real or not, the poem offers a location for the Geats
that does indeed require revision of Klaeber's map.

Klaeber offers the map only as a rough guide, however. In his text he
nods toward southwest Sweden as the land of the Geats ("Västergötland
is commonly believed to correspond to Hygelac's realm"), then dismisses
the problem by saying, "we are by no means compelled to believe that
the poet had very clear notions of the geography" (148). E. G. Stanley
reinforces that skepticism with his truism that it is a mistake "to understand literature not as invention contrived by art but as evidential
written matter."[8] Nevertheless, if inventions contrived by art are to com-
mand our suspension of disbelief, they ought to be internally consistent,
which often includes having a coherent, though not necessarily realistic,
sense of place. Just as fictional Huck floated sequentially down his real
Mississippi, the imaginary Beowulf might have sailed, as we did, from
the north down a real Cattegat Sea to Denmark, taking one to two days,
as the poem indicates, to reach his goal. Without seeking a Beowulfian
equivalent of Schliemann's wishful "mask of Agamemnon," without
even claiming that the poet's geographical sense was as specific as the

poem's, one can argue for this north to south direction of the journey from the way descriptions in the poem match or are related to real-world geography. It then follows that, if Beowulf is sailing down from the north, northward from Zealand must be his home.

The practical side of this book about places begins with Beowulf's journey to Denmark, the journey that Gillian and I so enjoyably "reinvented." The theory is simple, based on what the poem says about time and geography and the way tradition has located the ancient Danish dynasty of the Scylding kings near modern Roskilde. The poem has Beowulf and his friends sail from their homeland to Heorot, the royal hall of the Scyldings. They appear to have sailed across open sea for the last part of their journey, until they see the landmark of their destination:

> Wundenstefna   gewaden hæfde
> þæt ða liðende   land gesawon,
> brimclifu blican . . .

> The spiral-prowed (ship) had journeyed
> (to the point) that the seafarers saw land,
> sea-cliffs shining . . .
>
> *(Beowulf,* 220–22a)

This open sea route could only be taken from the north. This was the most exciting and persuasive fact I discovered by reading maps and talking to sailors. If the Geats had been navigating more conservatively along the coast, as was customary for the mariner in those days ("a 'rock-dodger,' steering from 'view to view,' and seldom out of sight of the land"; Marcus, 1980: 125), they would normally have hugged the Swedish mainland until they could see across the sound. They could have crossed over most easily where it is only three miles wide at Helsingör (more familiar to us as Elsinore), where Shakespeare adds to the otherwise flat landscape the "dreadful summit of the cliff / That beetles o'er his base into the sea" (*Hamlet* I, iv). Even without the advantage of that imaginary eminence, the melancholy prince could have had a view of Sweden from his castle ramparts.

Coastal navigation would have allowed the possibility that the Geatish mariners of *Beowulf* could be coming from any of a number of directions, but having them see the glitter of far-off cliffs marking their destination means they are approaching from open sea and thus necessarily from the north. Because the cliffs seen from sea in line 222 are matched by landmarks in the real world, the sea-cliffs marking the entrance to the fjords leading to Roskilde, I have suggested that the poet could have been familiar with certain "verbal sea-charts" of pilots and fishermen (Osborn, 1992), or he could have heard about the route from someone like King Alfred's informant Ohthere, or he might even have made the trip himself, poets not having been confined to one location then any more than now. The match between landscape and poem could also be coincidental; most commentators assume with Klaeber that the poet is simply adopting a formula about cliffs seen at the end of a sea journey (Clark, 1965).

Whether by coincidence or plan, it is a fact, despite Klaeber's skepticism about poetic sea-cliffs in general and those of Zealand in particular (xlvii), that when sailing across open sea from the north one does indeed see the cliffs of northern Zealand gleaming from afar, as Gillian has described so vividly. Along the coast from Gilbjerg Hoved to Spodsbjerg, marking the entrance to Isefjord and Roskilde Fjord that branches off it, these cliffs attain heights of thirty-four to forty-nine meters above the sea, not enormous but notable. Someone familiar only with the Copenhagen-Helsingör area, who had never seen that remote northern coastline and was struck by how Shakespeare exaggerated the setting for *Hamlet*, might well imagine Zealand as entirely flat. Whether Beowulf and his Geats are supposed to have seen the cliffs after a two-day trip like ours, with camping by night and then cutting across the open sea from the mainland, or after one long haul including an overnight run to arrive during the first hour of the next day (stellar navigation being possible in the fine weather implied by line 228), the open sea route to northern Zealand is the one they had to have taken if we are to accept information in the poem realistically, and this route with its timing suggests approximately where they must have set out.

Becoming increasingly intrigued by this logic of the text, I have made two *Beowulf* journeys with friends. The first was the sea voyage with Gillian in 1985 to test the hypothesis about Beowulf's sailing down from the north, and the second was by car in 1988 with Randolph Swearer, designer and head of the Department of Design at the University of Texas at Austin, to obtain photographs for *Beowulf: A Likeness*. The latter was a more encompassing land journey to all the major archaeological sites, including English ones, that could possibly be associated with the great Anglo-Scandinavian poem. My present account will now follow up the reenactive voyage of 1985, which Gillian has recounted in the first part of this chapter, with the Scandinavian part of the 1988 Beowulf journey with Randy. Beginning in the known and in general agreed-upon world of Beowulf's Danish exploits, we will then, with reference to details that support the location of Wedermark, follow Beowulf home to his own more mythical land as deduced and imagined from the poem. What follows is part travelogue, blessed by good weather and good companions, but also part scholarship intended to persuade, not so much about the poet's intended setting as the feasibility of the places in which we have chosen to imagine the actions of the poem.

About six miles outside the cathedral town of Roskilde, not far from the end of the long fjord into which Gillian and I sailed following the route we imagined for the Geats' coming to Denmark, lies the tiny hamlet of Gammel Lejre (also spelled Leire). After the sea voyage, Lejre must be the starting point of any further journey into the landscapes of *Beowulf*. When Randy and I came to visit this village that many scholars assume is the real-world site of imaginary Heorot, we chose to drive past the site to visit first the open-air museum located in nearby Herthadale, the museum I knew from the earlier journey with Gillian, when we had paid the brief visit that she mentions. Randy and I went there to get into the proper mood for the Iron Age, that period lasting in Scandinavia from about 500 B.C. to 800 A.D., after which the Viking Age began. The museum contains, among many other attractions of all periods, the reconstruction of a Germanic Iron Age village of around Beowulf's time, 500–600 A.D. During the summertime in this village, Iron Age "natives," with modern university degrees to authenticate their endeavors, studiously make Iron Age bread, and they have been known to set fire to the largest of the Iron Age halls to see how it burns. It burns down spectacularly. Although such reconstructive archaeology can be entertaining, the experiment was far less frivolous than I make it sound, because in ancient times burning a neighbor's hall down around his ears was the final reply to an insult real or imagined. If the Icelandic sagas are anything to go by, it was the destiny of a famous hall to be burned down. The *Beowulf* poet tells us that at the very moment the royal hall Heorot is raised, devouring flames of feud vengeance lie in wait sometime in the future (lines 81–83). The related Anglo-Saxon poem *Widsith* refers back to the battle at Heorot as a historic event: the Danes won, but "on this occasion, as is to be inferred from lines 82ff., the famous hall Heorot was destroyed by fire" (Klaeber, xxxv). In this context we found it fascinating to watch the film of a reenactive hall-burning, and then go from the lecture hall into the village to visit the restored Iron Age hall, restored both from the past and from the burning, ducking our heads to enter that low doorway.

Continuing past the village with its brightly thatched new hall and down the hill into the woods, we came suddenly upon the sacrificial bog, staked out with carcasses of horses fitted onto wooden frames and pointed across the dark water to hex unfriendly spirits, as in *Egil's Saga;* as Tacitus says, for the peoples of Germania "horses are the confidants of the gods" (chapter 10). Though we were not shadowed, as we stood there, by cliffs with overhanging frost-covered trees, it was easy to imagine Grendel's mother emerging from those fetid waters, and, even though prepared by past experience, I was startled again when Randy and I came suddenly upon those hex stakes, captured in Kate Breakey's haunting photograph in *Beowulf: A Likeness.* The way the diction in lines 1420–21 of *Beowulf* echoes that of lines 1635–39 persuades me that when Grendel's mother stakes out in her path the severed head of Æschere, the Dane she has killed in vengeance, she is meant to be using a heathen ritual similar to Egil's to repel the pursuing Geats and Danes—except that instead of a horse's head she uses the human one. When her foes come upon that head so suddenly, they are horrified at seeing their friend thus dishonored but also repelled and fearful at the monster-woman's ferocious magic.

In my personal mythology of time and place, and also according to the official Danish brochure (not necessarily accurate), the Herthadale site is older than the one at Gammel Lejre. Tacitus tells us that the ancient Germanic tribes worshiped a goddess named Nerthus (*Germania,* chapter 40), and the place-name Herthadale has been said to refer to the goddess Hertha, whose name is a variant of Tacitus's Nerthus, though recent scholarship casts doubt on this idea (Jones, 1984: 47). The public today tends to be attracted by ancient goddess or priestess figures (see Lefkowitz, 1993), and more than one modernizer has placed Grendel's mother herself in that sympathetic role. In any case, the wooded dale is apparently the site of an ancient heathen sanctuary, hence the token sacrificial bog.[9]

The more solid ground of Gammel Lejre lies some six kilometers to the east, and here we find physical evidence of a great prehistoric hall like that of the Scylding king Hrothgar, though this one was built several centuries after the mythical Heorot burned. In fact, there are a number of antiquities of interest here. The first landmark one sees is Hestebjerg, the "Hill of Horses" marked on the 1643 prospect map of Lejre by Olaus Wormius that Randy had the foresight to bring along (this map is reproduced in *Beowulf: A Likeness*). Upon this hill we actually did see a row of horses standing picturesquely against the skyline, much as they must have done in the seventeenth century and perhaps in Hrothgar's time as well.

Next we looked for the sign bearing quadruple loops, the Danish marker for a historical site, to point our way to the local ship-setting, a huge outline shape of a ship set out in stone. One of many in Scandinavia, it was perhaps a representative spirit ship intended to bear a slain warrior's soul to the land of the dead, as does Scyld Scefing's more authentically conceived ship in *Beowulf*. From *Ynglinga Saga* and *Skjoldunga Saga* Chambers quotes the accounts of "two ancient Swedish kings who, sorely wounded, and unwilling to die in their beds, had themselves placed upon ships, surrounded by weapons and the bodies of the slain. The funeral pyre was then lighted on the vessel, and the ship sent blazing out to sea" (1963: 68).[10] But building a stone-marked abstraction of a ship up here on the windy hilltop seems a starker, wilder custom than launching forth an actual ship upon the waves, laden with usable treasures for a future life "elsewhere." The real ship will go somewhere, if only to the bottom. The spectral ship makes the other world into a more distant, more metaphorical place.

Ritual, that most metonymic of acts joining people with their past and with the supernatural, might have brought that other world nearer. Perhaps in the bosom of this outline ship mourners built a pyre to burn the warrior with his equipment, watching the dark column of smoke go up into the clear sky as at the end of *Beowulf*. This is my afterthought in the gloom of the study. On the beautiful summer day when we were there, I drifted among the stones, counting the varieties of wildflowers growing in the grassy hold of the great ship. I found, among others, bluebells and cornflowers, huge lavender thistles, yellow feverfew (good against fevers), clover, shepherd's purse, yarrow (to increase the effect of ale), vetch, and dandelion puffs, the yellow dandelions having by this time of year turned silver. Walking there I wondered how many of the same flowers grew on this hilltop (barren then of ship) in Hrothgar's day, or whether a "real" Hrothgar and his queen had ever strolled together on these hills above their hall, speaking of things that mattered, like children and relationships with neighbors. I wondered whether their daughter Freawaru, after her angry husband Ingeld had burned her father's hall and perished there, had survived him to gather these flowers, some for use and others for beauty, her yellow hair turning gradually to silver.

That is only my daydream, but the battle between the Scylding kings and Ingeld the Heathobard, resulting in the hall-burning foreseen in *Beowulf*, appears to be rooted in tradition. In the poem *Widsith*, along with the names of the Danish king Hrothgar and his nephew Hrothulf, the hall Heorot is mentioned as the site of the battle with Ingeld and his Heathobards (lines 45–49, quoted by Klaeber, xxxv). The same battle seems to have been mentioned in the lost *Skjoldunga Saga* summarized centuries later (Garmonsway, 1968: 242) and also to have been the source of a poem recorded in Latin by the Dane Saxo Grammaticus around 1215 A.D. (ibid., 243–47). Much earlier, in eighth-century Northumbria, Alcuin refers to Ingeld and perhaps to his epic enmity with the Scyldings, when he scolds the story-loving monks of Lindisfarne: "Quid Hinieldus cum Christo?" ("What has Ingeld to do with Christ?"; ibid., 242). The Scyldings Hrothgar and Hrothulf are also named in numerous sources outside *Beowulf*, in chronicles, genealogies, histories like that of Saxo, and the sagas (see Garmonsway, 127–41, 155–206). In fact the nephew Hrothulf, a dubious friend to his uncle in *Beowulf*, has a saga to himself as the much-admired hero of *Hrolf Kraki's Saga*, in which his champion Bothvar Bjarki has certain affinities with Beowulf. Name changes are interesting here. Much as Anglo-Saxon Hrothulf becomes Norse Hrolf, Anglo-Saxon Hrothgar contracts to Norse Hroar, in Latin, Ro. So it is pleasant, though perhaps fanciful, to join Saxo in thinking of Roskilde as Ro's kilde, or spring, and the person thus commemorated as our own Hrothgar of *Beowulf*, that famous builder of halls. (It is more likely, however, that the *ros* of Roskilde is from *hross*, horse, as in such place-names of northern England as Rosgill, Rosley, and Ross Hall, and that the place-name antedates the great medieval city that grew up there, and its founder, perhaps a king at Lejre.) But the historical Danish kings who made Roskilde their seat of government, from which it eventually moved to Copenhagen, allowed the halls of Lejre to return to grass, forgotten.

Only a few years ago, in 1987, the archaeologist Tom Christensen of Roskilde Museum discovered under the grass at Gammel Lejre the site of an enormous hall probably of the tenth century, the largest prehistoric Germanic hall yet found. It is forty-eight meters long by eleven meters wide, nearly the size of an Olympic swimming pool. This is considerably larger than the great royal hall, about twenty-seven meters long, excavated in England at Northumbrian Yeavering, a hall that probably represents the kind that would have been familiar to our poet. Lejre's huge hall must have truly risen "heah ond horngeap" ("high and wide-gabled") to astonish all viewers, its carved gable horns lofty against the sky. Now we have news that another, older hall site, from around 800 A.D., has been revealed there, and evidence of an even earlier hall lies below that layer (*London Times*, February 14, 1992: 15).

Gammel Lejre itself does not feel nearly so Beowulfian as one might have hoped. In his edition of *Beowulf* Klaeber remarks sardonically, "Sarrazin claimed that the scenery of the first part of the *Beowulf* could be clearly recognized even in the present Lejre and its surroundings, while others (including the present editor) have failed to see more than a very general topographical resemblance" (xxxvii). Randy and I sympathized with this attitude. The landscape is so bland, so utterly devoid of epic grandeur, that earlier scholars were led to assert, like Wadstein, that the landscape descriptions in *Beowulf* "are purely fictitious, since they are obviously based on the kind of scenery that the poet was familiar with from his own native country" (273). Wadstein refers to Daniel H. Haigh's argument that the English poet imagined the Danish hall Heorot ("Hart") and the lake of the monsters in terms of landscapes around the northern English town Hartlepool, a thesis worthy of further examination, especially in view of Ekwall's (1960: 222) identification of Hartlepool, "the pool by Hart," with the place-name Heorot-ea in the Old English translation of Bede, circa 890 A.D. Nevertheless, as we walked in Denmark along Sarrazin's route over the moor and around the Stora Kattinge Sø—a lake that Sarrazin (1888: 8) identifies as "belonging to Grendel's domain," though he has the monster actually living in the inlet of the sea just beyond—we found the spatial relationships of this landscape satisfying and much like those suggested in the poem. After a leisurely three hours on foot, with various stops and side trips, we arrived at this lake of the monsters, now a separate body of water but in former days connected to the fjord. The Geats and Danes would have been quicker to reach it as they followed on horseback the bloody footprints of dying Grendel. When we arrived at the lakeside, I found the grassy sward so inviting and the lake so blue and calm that while Randy went back alone for the car I dozed off in the sun, exactly (to parody Sarrazin's *genau*) where Grendel and his mother were wont to roam. Even more disconcerting, or pleasing, depending on one's level of irony, a sanitorium with serene and well-kept grounds now stands in "the very place" where those two monsters used to rage and tear apart their victims for dinner.

Peter Bolwig, captain of the *Galadriel* and organic farmer, had invited us to a meal of a more civilized kind at his home in Sørø, which brought us to the southwest where we could visit Trelleborg. On this site stands the reconstruction of a great Viking Age hall, quite different from the lowly Iron Age halls we had visited at Herthadale. Though authorities now find many details wrong with its plan, the Trelleborg hall has a lovely air of freshness and space about it, and here we may actually see the curved gable horns branching out like the horns of a stag. The official brochure tells us that the hall is eight meters wide by fifteen meters long; the larger halls excavated at the same site are some three meters longer. The Trelleborg hall has stave-built walls of broad oak planks and a roof shingled like the stave churches of Norway; one of the original shingles was excavated during the dig. The outside gallery running around the building, based on the positions of posthole discolorations in the soil, is one of the details of construction that critics object to, suggesting instead that these posts were buttresses for the high walls. (The height of the walls is determined by the size and depth of the central pillars, that is, of their discolored holes.) Disregarding the archaeologists' quibbles, we found the hall of a friendly size for representing Heorot: fifteen meters' length was more comfortable than the nearly fifty meters of the hall at Gammel Lejre. The inside of the Trelleborg hall, pictured in *Beowulf: A Likeness,* is laid out like the hall interiors implied or described in the poem and the sagas, with broad benches fixed to the walls and the long fire built upon a central hearth from which the smoke escaped through roof vents raised like shutters. There are no windows.

While we were there, a sudden thundershower discouraged sightseers so that we were left alone in the hall. Randy was taking photographs while I sat with his equipment on one of the built-in benches, content. I thought of how in ancient times the warriors would sleep after their banquet on feather mattresses laid out upon such benches, and of how violent Beowulf's fight with Grendel must have been to tear these benches away from the sill of the hall onto which they were built (lines 775–76). But my thoughts were very idle. After a while, just as in the analogy for human life recorded by the Venerable Bede, a little bird—a swallow, not the Bedean and probably biblical sparrow—darted in at one door and out through another, in the space of time it takes an eye to twinkle. The bird flew from storm through the dry hall and back into summer storm, reminding us, as if our journey were not doing so with constant emphasis, of the mortality of all things earthly. A moment in the world, then flick! through the other door, no one knows whence or whither. But then I remembered that on leaving Lejre we had seen a double rainbow.

Trelleborg was our last scheduled stop in Denmark, and as we prepare now to depart this land, I should modify my earlier statement that spatial relationships there, even certain landscape features, accorded well with those suggested by the poem. Only the human landscape worked, the cliff-marked seacoast and the safe pastoral setting of the halls. When one thought of mountain-dwelling monsters, credulity failed. It would take a strong injection indeed from a horrific *Visio Pauli,* the literary source the poet is supposed to have drawn on for his purple descriptive passages (Klaeber, 183), to put the monsters and their appropriate scenery into this gently rolling landscape that lay dreaming and sunny when we visited it. The land we visited next was another story, however.

It is another story in *Beowulf* as well. The last third of the poem is as different in mood as green and rolling Denmark is different from my real-

world Wedermark of rock-hills and dark woods. Wedermark is a dragon-
land where monsters are thoroughly imaginable, where history is tragic,
and where treasure, as Gillian has observed, is real. I place it in Bohuslän
on the west coast of Sweden, between the "Geatish" river called the Göta
Älv and the river marking the modern Norwegian border, today called
the Glomma and formerly the Raum Älf or "Raum River," a name that
becomes important in the argument about Breca that follows.[11] In his
twelfth-century *Heimskringla,* Snorri Sturluson (1964: 48) says that this
land (in Snorri's time known as Ranríki) had formerly been called Alfheim, "river country," explaining that it was the land between these two
particular rivers.[12] Geologically, this land

> can be characterized as a level plain of primary rock, which is gently
> inclined to the west and gradually falls into an extensive archi-
> pelago. Typical of the landscape are the fissure valleys, filled with
> fertile, fine sediment, between often-bare mountain ridges. In the
> coastal zone the rocks may be covered by heather or juniper bushes
> or shrubs. In positions sheltered from the wind, in the slopes at the
> foot of the mountain ridges, can often be found small forests of oak,
> lime, elm, and hazel. In the Bronze Age these mixed-oak forests
> probably covered a much wider part of the landscape. The decid-
> uous trees have gradually been displaced by coniferous trees [plant-
> ed in recent times], which now cover extensive parts of the
> area . . . The bed-rock consists of granite . . . (Bertilsson, 1987: 26)

Off the densely skerried coast of this part of Bohuslän lie the two *väder* or
"windy" islands that are said to give the area its modern name, Väderöfjord, "Fjord of the Windy Isles" (Modéer, 1932: 142–44). I shall stan-
dardize this name in English as Weder Isle Fjord.

In a deeply personal way, quite irrespective of the romantic associations of the name, I found this landscape satisfying. It was a place I wanted to imagine as Beowulf's homeland, and in some remote way my own.
Even as I write now on a golden day in California, the sort of day that
everyone elsewhere longs for, copying out the description above has
filled me with nostalgia as I see in my mind's eye the bare granite hills
rising like islands above dense woods. The text of the poem itself permits
me to indulge my longing by appropriating this land as Beowulf's.

When early in the poem Beowulf and his companions arrive on Danish
shores to oppose the monster Grendel, the Dane guarding those shores
demands that these strangers tell him "whence your comings are" (line
257). Rather than answering in the geographical terms the question
seems to ask for, Beowulf replies with tribe and king: "We are Geats and

Hygelac's hearth-companions" (lines 260–61). Beowulf's answer satisfies the coastguard, who appoints men to look after their ship until it will take them back home again, as he says, "to Wedermark." So it appears that the guard recognizes from their ruler's name their identity specifically as Weder-Geats, perhaps distinct in some important way from the Geats in general, those Gautar who left their name in the provinces of Götland East and West.

Accepting the usual idea that the Geats were merely the generalized Gautar of Västergötland, I had planned our Geatish point of departure for Gillian's and my sea voyage on the basis of Klaeber's statement that the royal town of Beowulf's Geats had been "conjecturally located at Kungsbacka or at Kungälf (south and north of Göteborg respectively)" (xlviii). But sailing up the Cattegat from Denmark I had afterthoughts. Before we set off from Göteborg to sail south on our voyage proper, I spent some time below deck with my books and maps, especially giving attention to R. T. Farrell's tightly written arguments in *"Beowulf, Swedes, and Geats."* In this treatise Farrell includes a map (on which figure 3 here is based) showing the distribution in Sweden of major Iron Age treasures; he also indicates on that map the extent of probable Geatish (Gautar) territory. From this map and his plates I learned that an important sword hilt, closely similar in style to the Frankish sword decorated with garnet and gold found in the rich Anglo-Saxon ship burial at Sutton Hoo (see figure 5 and Farrell's plates 6 and 7), had been excavated in a burial mound at Hög Edsten in Bohuslän, halfway between Göteborg and Oslo. The place-name Hög Edsten was itself evocative in a way that reminds us of Tolkien: "High Oathstone" or even "The Howe of the Oath Stone." I wondered if there was an oath stone there. Despite Klaeber's remark that Bohuslän had possibly been part of the kingdom of Gautland (xlvii), however, Farrell had excluded that province from his map.

This district has always been what historians call a "debatable land," affiliated for all its recorded history now with one kingdom, now with another, and never attached firmly to any of its three great neighbors. When Ohthere described to King Alfred in the ninth century his sea journey down the Cattegat, he regarded this northern portion of the coast as part of Denmark (Lund, 1984: 22). Around the same time King Eirík of Sweden won the territory and assigned it to "Hrani the Gautish" to rule; *Heimskringla* records that "his domain extended from the Svína Sund to the Gaut Elf River. He was a powerful earl"(70). But Harold Fairhair gained it back, perhaps in the 880s, for Norway. In later years it again belonged to Sweden, and so on. The language now spoken there is a dialect

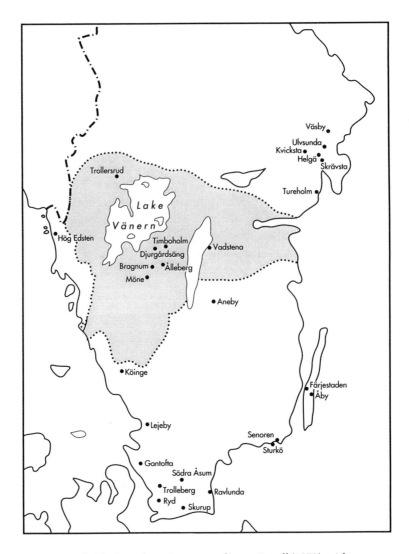

Figure 3. Probable Geatish territory according to Farrell (1972), with treasure burials circa 400–550 A.D.

hovering between Norwegian and Swedish. In other words, what we now know as Bohuslän is the marginal sort of territory that the term "debatable land" implies, a land only loosely identified with a particular centralized or national authority. Its name means "farmhouse district," reinforcing its agricultural hence disempowered status, and it is one of those countries, or rather noncountries, that evokes an area of nondefinition on a map.

Perhaps that is why Farrell excluded it from Geatland. Even this exclusion has its interest, however. If we are to regard the suggestion in the poem as correct that these particular Geats were to be driven from their land once their powerful king had died, then the likeliest land for Wedermark is one where later records suggest there were no Geats (or Gautar). Moreover, the "debatable" status of the area through much of its recorded history offers a possible explanation for the association of Beowulf's king Hygelac alternatively with the Geats and the Danes in the works outside the poem that mention his raid upon the Frisians.[13] Similarly, in the Scandinavian traditions corresponding to the Geatish-Swedish wars in *Beowulf*, "the Danes have stepped into the place originally occupied by the Geats" (Klaeber, xliii). Leake (1967: 122–26) has claimed (and Niles agrees) that these conflicting associations prove that Hygelac, along with his Geats, never existed. An alternative explanation might be that these conflicts merely point to the fact that the territory itself, once inhabited by a group at feud with the Swear and ruled by Hygelac or someone of a similar name, had different national (or tribal) affiliations at different times.[14] Assigning the debatable territory of Weder Isle Fjord to Hygelac alleviates the ambiguity of his nationality if not quite resolving the issue.

Another problem in the poem that may be solved or eased by placing Beowulf's homeland at this location is the distance he and Breca swam or, as Fred Robinson (1974) and others suggest, rowed in their boyhood exploit of which we have Unferth's and Beowulf's own versions (lines 504–83a). While on the sea, they are driven apart by storm and Breca is cast ashore on the Heatho-Reamas' land, from which he makes his way home (lines 518–23a). Commentators have associated Breca's landfall with modern Romeriki, formerly Raumaríki, the Norwegian province north of Oslo (Klaeber, 148; see also his map), but this is an inland province. The river Raum, called Glomma on modern maps, that drains this land empties into Svina Sound, the border between modern Norway and Bohuslän, which suggests that the land of the Heatho-Reamas (Old English Ream corresponding to Old Norse Raum) may have extended much farther south than where modern Romeriki now lies, to include the seashore at the river's outflow. Beowulf comes ashore on *finna land* (line 580), which earlier editors assumed meant the land of the Finnish Lapps or Finmarken in northern Norway and more recent editors (following Schück) have connected with Finnheden in southwest Sweden—though C. L. Wrenn (1958: 311) stretches a point when he says that this place "could have been reached within human possibility by Beowulf from Geatland" (placing Geatland around the Göta Älv).

By reinterpreting the onomastic evidence, one can realign the

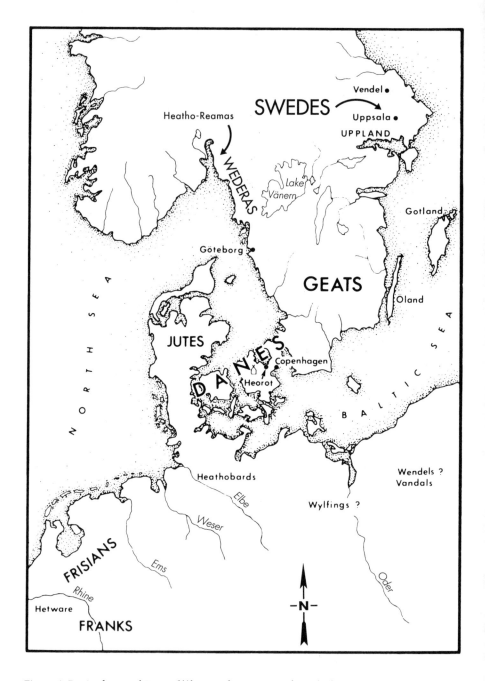

Figure 4. Revised map of *Beowulf* (from Osborn, 1983, after Klaeber; emended 1993).

emphasis of the story so that the geography makes better sense (see the revised map of *Beowulf* in figure 4). The element *fin* often means "wood" in place-names, and it could serve here as a descriptive term referring to the wooded terrain of Beowulf's own land, or perhaps to the driftwood thrown up on those stormy shores of Weder Isle Fjord, rather than to the far northern territory of the Finns or even Finnheden (Osborn, 1989). Even as a proper noun *Finna Land* need not imply great distance. Sarrazin (1888: 32) long ago pointed to the place-name "Finnsland" near Lysekil in Bohuslän.[15] One does not have to agree with him that this place-name is identical to that of the poem to argue that the account of the boys' exploit makes better sense if we understand *finna land* as local to Wedermark and conceive of the Heatho-Reamas of the river Raum and the Weder-Geats of Weder Isle Fjord as neighboring tribes (compare Swanton, 1978: 192). This reading saves young Beowulf hundreds of miles of wearisome swimming (or rowing) and concentrates attention upon the monster-killing that seems to be the point of his telling the story.

In a cautious consideration of various possibilities for Beowulf's homeland, R. W. Chambers (1963: 342) refers to the Weder Isles, as did a number of scholars before him [see Cosijn, 1991 (originally 1892): 33, 97]. On our 1985 trip, not knowing then of Sarrazin's interest in the area, I noticed that these islands lay parallel on the map to treasure-bearing Hög Edsten. Intrigued by this association of place-name and treasure, I went up on deck and suggested to my sailing companions that we should take time out to rent a car in Göteborg and go there. They were delighted to chase my wild geese with me, and we had a lovely day, stopping at the old schoolhouse at Hög Edsten and being led by the summer guest, in the absence of the owner Jan Ekborg, to a pile of rocks in the woods that she assured us was where the sword had been discovered. That pile was, we found out later, the registered ruin of a neolithic dolmen, quite suitable except for its inland location for the dragon's rich and enchanted lair, but unlikely as the site of Iron Age treasure. As we left, Gillian and I noticed the little howe out by the side of the road, which we learned later was where the sword had actually been found (by Johannes Svensson on October 15, 1863, according to Montelius, 1880: 212). The summer guest told us that the area was rich in long-ago graves that the schoolteacher knew more about than she did. "You really should talk to him," she urged. But we had to get back to Göteborg, to eat dinner and sleep and start early in the morning on our voyage to Heorot, the purpose of our trip to Scandinavia.

When I returned to Hög Edsten with Randy in 1988, the first person we encountered was the retired high-school teacher Jan Ekborg. Lanky and smiling, Jan entered immediately into the spirit of what we were doing, first setting us right about the dolmen and the mound, then, as a geologist, explaining the strange smooth hole I had noticed in the mountainside behind his house. It had been made by an Ice Age glacier, which had rubbed a stone around and around to drill a pit two meters across and five meters deep, straight down into the granite, with a bend near the bottom. He had drained and measured it once, he told us. But then he smiled and added that, personally, he thought it had something to do with dragons. "There is a dragon in *Beowulf*," I remarked, thinking, however, that the pit would accommodate only a baby, not Beowulf's fifty-foot monster. But Jan was delighted with the connection, and that horrible hole has been "the dragon nest" ever since, where *she* (of course) lays her eggs. "Whoosh!" he exclaims to visitors, indicating with sweep of hand and head how Beowulf's dragon blasted it out with *her* fiery breath.

Jan is not the only person in that area to amuse himself with fantasies about dragons. Sarrazin points to the nearby place-name Dragsmark (compare Wedermark), the site of a ruined monastery. He cites a local folktale that explains the name by the presence of a dragon that guards a silver cup (*silfverskål*) within the hill called the Skålberg, and he points out that the *Beowulf* dragon was awakened by the theft of just such a cup (1888: 34). As he observes in his footnote, this is a romantic dale. But I suspect that despite the folktale the place-name has more to do with dray horses than dragons (a dragon being *orm* or *drake* in Swedish).

Later, more serious in reply to my further questioning, Jan told us that he knew of no oath stone. He does know, however, the name and nature of the flowers in his woods and is able to name many of them in English and Latin as well as Swedish. He gathers mushrooms to eat and neither dies nor goes berserk; he showed me the red, spotted ones that the Vikings supposedly ate for battle fervor, the "berserker rage" (see Lincoff and Mitchell, 1977: 77–99). He knows how the Ice Age glaciers shaped the granite outcroppings that rise above the woods and the fields of grain like huge floating ships or icebergs of stone, and, best of all for our purposes, he knows the antiquities of the area. I do not believe we could have found a better resource person even if we had carefully sought one out, instead of stumbling upon Jan because he lives at Hög Edsten.

Of course he is not a Geat, though, much as we would like him to be one. The Geats, like their dragon, are gone. That is one thing the poem is about. After a fugitive has taken a goblet, perhaps a *silfverskål*, from the sleeping dragon's hoard, the monster awakens, misses his cup, and angrily swoops down by night upon the royal hall, which is standing empty as in peaceful times the warriors sleep elsewhere. Like many another northern seeker of vengeance, the monster sets the hall ablaze, burning to cinders "the stronghold of the people," *ealond utan* (lines 2333b–34a). The descriptive term *ealond* has puzzled commentators for more than a century. Cosijn [1991 (originally 1892): 97] suggested that it need not "be taken in its restrictive meaning" (island), which later on became the usual one. In fact, in the place-name Heorot-ea, already mentioned, the -ea element refers "no doubt to the headland or peninsula on which Hartlepool stands" (Ekwall, 1960: 222). This is how I would imagine Beowulf's royal hall, on a headland or eminence overlooking the sea; earlier in the poem we were told that Hygelac was waiting for Beowulf "at home with his companions near to the seawall" (lines 1923–24a).

That stronghold lies in ruins after the monster's attack and the people are terrorized, so Beowulf, an elderly king but still the monster-slayer, goes out to confront the dragon. Aided by his young kinsman Wiglaf, he succeeds in killing him, but in doing so is mortally wounded. As Beowulf lies dying, Wiglaf brings out some of the treasure from the dragon's lair, and the old king rejoices that he could win it for his people. After he is dead, in what I see as an extravagant gesture as loving and suicidal as Beowulf's own, his loyal people honor him by placing the dragon's gold in his burial mound—"as useless to men as it was before," the poet laments (line 3168). With no more treasure, no king, and surrounded by enemies, the Weder-Geat warriors are doomed to death in battle and the women will "walk in an alien land" (lines 3015–19). What land? Where did those women's voices carry their story, that it might be appropriated in years to come?

Randy and I spent our first few days at Hög Edsten exploring and photographing the major Germanic Iron Age monuments of the area, monuments that are on the whole neglected by tourists and archaeologists alike in favor of the amazing and charming, and outrageously phallic, Bronze Age rock carvings, found more densely here than anywhere else in Sweden, or indeed in the world, it is claimed. Each of us had seen and photographed the rock carvings in previous summers, and we were ready now for the Iron Age monuments of Wedermark. After our local mound, Jan's howe (which though small is the site of the richest treasure find in the area), the first antiquity we visited was the nearest *domarring* marked on the map, a ring of twenty-two stones in which judgments or "dooms" (*domar*) were decreed. This was the prettiest Iron Age site that we saw. Dark spruces surrounded a sunny, grassy sward that was cleared in the middle of the ring of stones, and a wild rosebush grew there among the other wildflowers, perhaps above the grave that had yielded, among burned bones in a pottery urn, a bone comb, molten glass from a drinking vessel, and a whetstone; archaeologists date these finds to about 600 A.D. It was curious how gentle and welcoming that doom ring seemed to us, when horrible rites may once have been celebrated there and fateful judgments almost certainly pronounced (for examples of grisly results of such "dooms," see note 9 of this chapter).

Later we went to the gravefields of Grebbestäd, where a great number of mounds had been raised together in a large field. Many of these were crowned with *bauta* stones, solitary unmarked standing stones to commemorate the dead. In some parts of Sweden such stones bear runic inscriptions, but there is a great dearth of such inscriptions in Bohuslän. If the tribes that once lived here were Beowulf's people, or a Geatish subgroup that the poet assigns to Beowulf, their lives were not graced with literacy.

The final site of importance that Randy and I visited, during a thunderstorm, was the thickly scattered gravemounds on the wooded hilltop at Vrångstäd. Here we realized that there could be monsters in the woods and that the dead very probably walked as well. Throughout our trip I had been talking about sleeping on a mound one night in the hope of getting dream inspiration from the dweller therein, a custom mentioned in the sagas and akin to Cædmon's experience in the cowshed, where a dream helper brought him our earliest recorded English poem. But here at Vrångstäd I abruptly went quiet about that idea, later to be resurrected in Iceland in another story context. Not even if I could learn in a dream the truth about the Weder-Geats would I sleep on those ominous mounds. They were, as Randy observed, "aggressive graves." Fitting monuments, I decided, for those Iron Age Wederas who may have brought about their own demise as a people by such unwarranted aggression as King Hygelac's piratical raid in which he was slain—and launched into written history.

Other accounts (see note 13 of this chapter) support and supplement the four different passages in *Beowulf* that refer to this raid: lines 1202–14, 2354–66, 2501–8, and 2913–21. According to the Dutch scholar Godfrid Storms, it was probably in 523 A.D. that Hygelac and his warriors attacked and at first defeated the Hetwares, a tribe on the Rhine, but when support came for the enemy the battle turned and Hygelac was slain by a Frankish warrior named Dayraven. Beowulf in turn killed his lord's slayer as duty required, escaping then with "thirty items of battle gear" (lines 2359–62; see Robinson, 1965, for this interpretation).[16] Could the gold and garnet-adorned Frankish sword of Hög Edsten, dated between 500 and 550 A.D., be a treasure that someone brought home to Hygelac's land from that documented raid? Or were rich Frankish swords

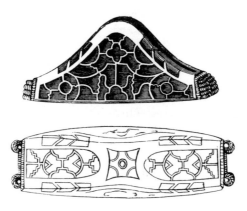

Figure 5. Frankish sword hilt found at Hög
Edsten (from Montelius, 1880: 212).

simply the fashionable accoutrement with which to be buried in those days? Was it a last treasure of a disappearing dynasty?

That part of the poem set in the homeland of the tribe specified as Weder-Geats or Wederas, unique to *Beowulf*, is packed with references to tribal history, including the great battle against the Sweon (the "Swedes" of Vendel in eastern Sweden). If those Swedes and Geats are located east and west instead of north and south, the references to the battle taking place "over the sea" (lines 2380 and 2394) no longer present a problem, because Lake Vänern now lies between. Confirming these locations is the important winter battle on the ice of this enormous lake, referred to in various sources outside the poem. *Ynglinga Saga*, for example, reports it or a similar battle between the Norwegian King Ali of Uppland and Swedish Athils, who correspond to the kings Onela of the Sweon and Eadgils the Geat in *Beowulf*; approximately the same geographical directions are involved, with the principal characters' homelands reversed.[17] All these variants on events presented as historical in the poem suggest that the poet might have known about or even invented an offshoot branch of Geats or Gautar, called Wederas, who established a small and perhaps fleeting colony along this windy coast, built forts and mounds, made foolhardy attacks on stronger neighbors, and thereby got themselves destroyed as a cultural entity sometime around the mid-sixth century, just as the woman prophesying at the end of the poem foresees. After the disappearance of this people, the memory of these events recorded in Scandinavian texts usually assimilates the Weder-Geats to the Danes or, as in that fight on the ice, the Norwegians.

Opinions differ regarding the implications of the prophecy of the Geatish woman at Beowulf's funeral (lines 3153–55, reinforcing 2910–

3027) and how seriously it may be taken. Fred Robinson has recently pointed out that

> a woman prophesying (accurately) the doom of a people is itself a recurring motif in the annals of the Germanic people . . . It is important to note the Germanic cultural background of the prophesying woman at the close of *Beowulf,* for some scholars have not given sufficient weight to her words and have even doubted whether the *Beowulf* poet intended us to understand that the Geatish nation is doomed following the death of Beowulf. (1988: 244–45)

R. T. Farrell, however, proclaims it is "a realistic view"

> that the Gautar were gradually dominated by the Svear, and that they were gradually subsumed into the larger kingdom of Sweden, while maintaining their cultural identity in many respects. This process was not completed until well after A.D. 1000. (1972: 270)

Historically speaking, it seems that the prophesied fall of Beowulf's tribe, if this tribe was the usual Gautar, must have occurred centuries after the fictional date of his death. Yet the discrepancy in dates and the opposition of the two views evaporate if one simply removes Beowulf's Weder-Geats from the major Svear-Gautar political scene as represented on Klaeber's map and understands the woman's prophecy to apply specifically to the marginalized, in every sense debatable, kingdom of Wedermark.

This kingdom, its hero, and its fall after his death may all be an invention woven from bits of northern history and myth, perhaps to create dynastic origins much as genealogies do (see Sisam, 1953). But the correspondence of places in Bohuslän to the poem is evocative, calling us to believe in the poem's geographical "truth." Could the poem *Beowulf* be, among other things, an elegy for a people who lived near modern Fjällbacka, a town that takes its name from the mighty cliffs that dominate it? Are these the *Geata clifu* of line 1911 recognized as home by the young warriors returning from Denmark? One can well imagine the *bat under beorge* ("boat at the foot of the mountain," line 211) waiting in this harbor when they set out earlier. On the top of this same mighty and truly beetling rock stands an ancient cairn that seafarers used as a landmark until recently; it is marked on the topographical map of the area with the runic R signifying that it is a recognized ancient monument (see plate 1). This cairn recalls Beowulf's dying request at lines 2802–8 for a landmark by the sea to be called "Beowulf's *Beorg.*" A place-name of this

Figure 6. Engraving of cairn (from Huyshe, 1907).

kind does exist (in addition to the questionable Bigulfesburh mentioned by Dorothy Whitelock, 1951: 66): the landmark mountain at the head of Iceland's Seydisfjord called Bjólfsfell, "Bjólf's Mountain," named after an early settler there from "Thuluness in Foss" (*Landnámabók*, 289–90). (Old English Beowulf contracts to Old Norse Bjólfr, just as Old English Hrothulf contracts to Old Norse Hrólfr.) Even though the Geatish hero who bears that name may be a myth, the early settler's name is real, and his former home is most likely to be identified as the Foss or Fors several times mentioned in *Heimskringla*, the "Fors in the Ranríki district" (Hollander translation of *Heimskringla*, 717) that is at one point firmly located near the Bohuslän river Befja that "empties into the sea at the present town of Uddevalla" (781, note)—about one half hour by car from Hög Edsten.[18] "Beowulf" is also recorded as a real name in the north of England as early as the seventh century (Garmonsway et al., 1968: 91); it does not appear at all, so far as I know, in the Danish or Swedish records. I am not arguing that the hero was real, merely that the name itself is real and occurs, in at least one important case, in a context that seems to be associated with Bohuslän, more specifically with the Weder Isle Fjord, our "Wedermark."

The poem itself may be the greatest monument ever raised to a Germanic hero, and this has implications for the imagined ancestral origins of the Anglo-Saxon audience for whom the poet composed. One might imagine that the Weder-Geats never did die out completely. The Geatish messenger predicts that after the inevitable battles following Beowulf's death the women will be doomed "to walk sadly, bereft of their gold, in an alien land" (lines 3018–19). At this new home perhaps those that made up the remnant of the tribe called themselves by another name, a name associating them with a striking feature of the new land just as the name Wederas did with the wild weather of the old. Yet pursuing that thought stretches the line of romantic speculation too far, beyond the bounds of the possibilities sought here. Better to leave the Wederas afloat, as the poet does, in history and myth, merely imagining them in their boats moving beneath the notable *beorg* of their homeland, identified by us in search of bearings with that great cliff of Fjällbacka, as they set out for a harbor hardly more certain than Scyld's in his ship of death.

After Randy had gone back to the United States, after the Weder-Geats had sailed away (that is, when I had tentatively finished this essay), Jan Ekborg and I went walking in the woods across the valley, woods that he had known for thirty years without stumbling on their secret. We were led there by a sentence in a book and a neighboring farmwife's memory of long-ago courtship. Overgrown with birch and fir trees so as to be invisible from the farm track, gravemounds rose, a hidden wooded field of small barrows, each topped with a heavy boulder to mark the grave—or to hold the grave dweller down. Dark in a copse of pines near to those graves, like a giant nail holding Iron Age culture firm, we found what must surely be the ancient oath stone of Hög Edsten. It stood sunken in leafmeal and surrounded by the nine stones of a doom ring, marking the sacred ceremonial council site where, in those ancient days, local treaties were sealed and chieftains were sworn to rule their people justly. Laying my hand on the cool rock, rough with lichen and age, I wondered: Whose hand last was laid on this stone to swear?

Saint Augustine, who tells us so much about how to read medieval texts, imposes three safeguards on interpretation. First, as Judith Ferster (1986: 151) explains his method, each reader "must try to discover the author's intentions . . . this is good faith interpretation." Second, each must "recognise the partiality" of the personal view, "that it is not complete and that he [or she] loves it because it is his [or her] own." Third, the truth that a person finds in a passage "must be consistent with the truth obtained from other sources." Although Augustine's goals are quite different from ours, his being the Christian interpretation of Scripture, his method calls for much the same awareness of and allowance for a reader's faithful but alert partiality that Gillian and I share in this book about the landscape of our desire. "It is not a historical landscape which here surrounds us," says Gwyn Jones, writing of Scandinavian legendary history, "and should not be regarded as such" (1984: 8). Nevertheless, what mountaineer David Craig says of dangerous, compelling climbs is also true of the homelands of legendary heroes: "You know they are there, they lurk in the world's fastnesses, actual but also with something of a dream status—images you entertain in advance of the experience, which feel so alive that they become magnets, attracting you half-reluctant into their reality" (1987: 70).

Perhaps Wedermark, homeland of Beowulf and his dragon, can legitimately claim nothing but a dream status. Yet, in the secret fastness of my heart, I know I have been there.

CHAPTER 2

Geography in the Reader

Place in Question

The places and questions examined in this chapter come largely from our observations and experiences traveling in Iceland. We set out with some specific academic goals and, of course, some conceptual maps in our minds. I (Gillian) had received a grant to develop a new course, and as part of the process of amassing teaching materials we planned to visit and photograph sites of five well-known sagas (those of Egil, Njal, Laxdæla, Hrafnkel, and Grettir). One express purpose was to consider the realism of the geographical and historical information in the sagas. Our hypotheses and aims, however, were changed and expanded—as they had been on our *Beowulf* voyage—by the actual experience of the Icelandic landscape. When I returned I recall writing an elaborate explanation to the grants committee of why and how my original proposal differed so markedly from the account of the experience. "Iceland is a place to meet the unexpected, especially in the form of weather," I wrote, acutely conscious of both cliché and understatement. There was much that we could not have predicted.

When we set out on the main ring road, we found the going slow and difficult; the road, completed just eighteen years ago, is only 30 to 40 percent paved as yet, and much of it was under repair after a bad winter's erosion. We understood why car rental rates in Iceland are three or four times the European standard. Not only did we travel at a much slower speed than anticipated because of extremes of weather and road conditions, we discovered upon exploring and talking to Icelanders many more saga sites than we had supposed existed. Many historical sites are unmarked. Icelanders are traditionally both interested in and informed about the island's history and literature, and we often found people eager to share their own theories about controversial points, and to show or direct us to saga locations. Broadly speaking, place-names and farm locations have not changed a great deal since saga times, and we already had

Figure 7. Map of Iceland with our saga sites.

much to photograph and research that could be easily and directly corroborated in the literature.[1] What has changed in some instances, however, is the shape of the landscape; several farms in *Njal's Saga*, for example, had been destroyed by the shifting glacial sands or volcanic movements.[2] We were staying for the most part at remote farmhouses where the farmers could tell us local history and legend, and identify landscape formations—a gully, a rock, a ridge with a particular shape or characteristic—that are described but not named in the literature.

Faced with this welter of new and unexpected present information, we were obliged to reexamine and reformulate some of the questions we had been asking of the past. We had been interested in the issues of authenticity and historicity in the sagas, and in the way these issues might inform ongoing debate about the oral or literary origins of the saga form. Indeed, one of the most tangible results of the trip was the developing ability to gauge the degree of historical and geographical fact in the sagas, to determine whether the saga writer knew his material personally or by hearsay, the degree to which landscape descriptions were exact down to the very shape of a meadow, and whether they were collocations or distortions of varieties of landscape, or complete fictions. In the northeastern dales of *Laxdæla Saga,* for example, it was possible to find "the very place" where Kjartan could have died, and where Gudrun might have watched the murder of her husband Bolli. (I will return to this idea of exactitude—the "Eureka impulse" discussed in the Introduction—and the exciting illusion it generates in the "Places in Question" section of this chapter.) One could also hypothesize that the writer of *Grettir's Saga,* unlike the writer of *Laxdæla Saga,* might not have been a local man. The waterfall into which the hero Grettir threw a troll woman turned out to be a mere hillside gill, but this was only fifteen or so kilometers from Góðafoss, one of the most dramatic waterfalls in Iceland, which raised the possibility that this comparatively inexact use of landscape represented a form of poetic license and bespoke a "literary" intention. Marijane discusses these questions and the idea of "place in translation" in the final section of this chapter.

This present, more literal experience of landscape inscribed in a medieval past and text gave rise to other questions: What happens to the reader's previous "literary" perspective when new visual information is introduced, and how is the reader involved or implicated in this realization of the text? What kinds of processes are involved in this visual negotiation with the past, in the re-creation or reinvention of literal and literary place? To what extent has our study produced a different story, another saga of a saga?

This last question was thrown into even more specific relief by our additional reliance on nineteenth-century Icelandic scholar and watercolorist W. G. Collingwood. *Pilgrimage to the Saga-Steads of Iceland,* published in 1899 and coauthored by Jón Stefánsson, is a written and visual record of their journey by horse. This provided valuable information and shortcuts to finding many saga sites, while Collingwood's stunning paintings also provided a filtering lens, another place of negotiation with the text and the past. In some instances, then, we were chasing at least three visions, three perceptions of space and place: Collingwood's, our own, and the saga's.

I had initially organized this chapter so that I would look first at some specific places, and then at some specific selves in place, although this division will become increasingly arbitrary as issues concerning places (both literal and literary) and selves (whether fictional or medieval or modern) overlap and reflect on each other. My attempts to disentangle selves from places, to theorize one without the other, or to theorize a dialectic where one informs the other, lead me around (and back) to some recurrent and current critical issues, and I think these warrant some

41

further investigation, though necessarily general and brief, before I return to—and modify—my original plan.

"Place" is an oddly misleading word: it frames, or would seem to demand, a picture, a space enclosed within a frame. Theorists as different as D. C. D. Pocock, Jim Wayne Miller, and Yi-Fu Tuan would agree that the nature of place, having a sense of place, is above all a process of situating the self, of negotiating and integrating information on many levels. Far from being static, then, place presupposes a good deal of activity. Pocock would argue that our way of seeing and perceiving place, indeed "our cognitive frame of reference for viewing reality" (1981: 13), is certainly a cultural, and might also be a largely literary, construction. Oscar Wilde's assertion that "the nineteenth century, as we know it, is largely an invention of Balzac" rings true for Pocock, in that it pinpoints with glib assurance the vital connection between familiar or received cultural or literary forms, and present perception, the ways in which the past creates and ordains pictures in the present.

When I think here specifically of our visual, intellectual, and emotional connection to Collingwood's work, Wilde's comment seems much less of a cliché. I also recall C. S. Lewis's consuming passion for "northernness" in spite of the fact that he never felt the urge to travel northward. Helen Gardner (1965: 420) describes how he becomes infatuated with the idea via literary and musical influences, chief among which was Wagner's *Ring*. In a discussion of regionality, Miller (1987: 3) states that "what we choose to think of as regions are mental constructs bearing little relation to geography or history"; instead, they function as arenas for self-definition via rejection and inclusion of the places and spaces of others. In Tuan's view place is a complex synthesis of cultural, experiential, and environmental attitudes, and the experience and definition of place become an intersubjective reality where self and place cocreate each other. Such a view requiring that we include the self's role in the creation of landscape resonates with further complexity when we are considering medieval selves and places from a present perspective.

Even this limited sampling of critical views suggests that the literature of place (ideas of place, being in place, having a sense of place) can be an interdisciplinary forum for questions about divisions and relations between self and other that have preoccupied some areas of poststructuralist criticism. To look at the relationship between the perceiver and that which is perceived in terms of place is also to resurrect and reconfigure old questions about the nature of the aesthetic. Cultural geographers and theorists of place have moved in several directions from Wordsworth and Dewey's point of insistence that "beauty" is discovered in the unifying relationship between the individual observer and the environment observed, that is, in the experience of landscape, in the coming together of the half-perceived and half-created elements of the experience of landscape.

The composition of this mysterious point of unity has been deconstructed by varieties of emphasis on the observing self or on the observed other, on the nature and the role of the subject in the creation of the aesthetic, or on the created object. The analyses of the individual's connection to landscape have led environmentalists and geographers to examine analogous animal behavior and its territorial or self-protective motivations, and to consider the physical dimensions of our connection to landscape. One view, loosely called the "prospect-refuge" theory, would parallel the human observer's relationship to a perceived environment with the creature's relationship to habitat, a process of surveying a landscape in terms of its potential to fulfill needs and provide satisfactions: "The creature exploring is always potentially the creature escaping" (Appleton, 1975: 71), always seeking out whether or how it "belongs" in a place. The idea of landscape as refuge took on some startling new dimensions for me in the context of certain Icelandic prospects, or vistas, especially those inhabited by the outlaw Grettir. These were places that might reject, encompass, or overwhelm self. How place might resituate, or even reconstitute, self will be taken up in my discussion of Grettir in the "Selves in Place" section of this chapter.

We have a fundamentally physical, bodily relationship with the land, Tuan and others would argue, and from this basis we construct its meaning. How we perceive and organize space, and how we relate to place, are grounded in two kinds of essential facts: "the posture and structure of the human body, and the relations (whether close or distant) between human beings" (Tuan, 1977: 34). Many aspects of spatial description (high and low, front and back, near and far, and so forth) have both physically and culturally evaluative connotations; Tuan calls attention to the many ways in which language reflects body/space connection. Folk measurements, for example, often reflect body parts or functions, as in a "handful," a "foot," a "stone's throw," or "within shouting distance." He asks that we consider the spatial implications of a phrase like "we are close friends," or the self/other split in spatial language indicated by the parallels of we = here, they = there, and hence "us" set against "them" (50).

When Tuan equates estimates of longer distance with the experience of greater physical effort—with how much land may be sown or traversed in a day, for instance (45)—or recalls the British custom of "beating the bounds," where the parish priest literally marks out boundaries and so claims church jurisdiction by hitting certain markers with a stick (176), he evokes the palpable connections of the details of our lives with the spaces we inhabit. Two images come to my mind here, one a desperate image from the past, the other an irreverent one from the present. When we were staying at a farmhouse in southern Iceland, the farmer told us a story about her farm's history that was well known and rehearsed locally, although it had reputedly occurred over one hundred years ago. The present relations between this farmer's family and the neighbors were very strained. All the neighbor children were hostile, and even the dog was extremely unfriendly. Explaining this apparent continuation of the saga principle of feud, the farmer told us that although such tensions often came about when farms were so close together, the enmity between these two farms had been inherited. In the later part of the nineteenth century the daughter of the neighboring farmer had become pregnant, presumably out of wedlock; her father made a bargain with her to provide for the child, granting her as much land as she could walk around while in labor. That was the reason for the comparatively small size of our host's farm.

Such stories, true or not, are "treatments of space," revealing "operations on places" (de Certeau, 1984: 122), which in turn disclose the many ways in which narratives can literally intersect our lives, position us; they are part of the "oral narration that interminably labors to compose spaces, to verify, collate and displace their frontiers" (123). The woman laboring to create her space parodically recalls in my view Michel de Certeau's analogy of the judge, whose activity in deciding territorial claims coincides with the creation of narrative: "Genealogies of places, legends about territories. Like a critical edition, the judge's narration reconciles these versions" (122). As the judge is primarily engaged in the operation of marking out boundaries, he is retelling cultural stories that have determined and articulated spaces, as well as our physical and legal relation, enforced or enforcing, to those spaces.

Contemporary comedienne Roseanne Barr (now Arnold) evokes the second image that interests me in her discussion of some stereotypical attitudes toward women and space, i.e., that women do not have a sense of direction and cannot read maps. She concedes the latter point, "because only the male mind could conceive of one inch equaling a mile" (Barr, 1986). Both images that I have presented are stereotypic—one shows us extreme victimization and female impotence, the other pokes fun at masculine delusions of extreme potency—but stereotypes often derive their power from some point of validity. The first story is not paralleled but at least echoed in *Hauksbók*, a version of the Icelandic *Book of Settlements, Landnámabók:* a woman could claim "only as much land as she could walk around, while leading a two-year-old well-fed heifer, from dawn to sunset on a spring day" (Byock, 1988: 56). A man could claim "an area no larger than he and his crew could carry fire over in a single day" (55). The sagas have plenty to say about the second analogy. Even the mighty hero Grettir is called to task by a serving woman about the size of his penis. His response—to rape the woman—makes some new sense out of Barr's "joke."[3] Although "the boastful slut may well be right" (*Grettir's Saga,* chapter 75), Grettir asserts that size is not the issue, but rather the masculine prerogative of strength and possession. Grettir both confounds and reinforces the stereotypical connections between penis size and masculine effectiveness, and we shall see that many other areas of his behavior confuse expectation and raise contradiction. Grettir aside, however, my overall point here is that these gender-specific images of connections of self to space reveal an intimate level of bodily inscription. We map our world, our spaces and places, with our bodies, even as our body is inscribed by them.

The process of inscription reveals the dialectical relationship between what Pierre Bourdieu calls the "habitat," the immediate physically and socially structured environment, and the "habitus," the collective symbolic codes that order the experience of its members. Bourdieu maps this dialectic onto and through gender-related divisions of labor and space in his analysis of Berber society:

> For example, the opposition between movement outwards towards the fields or the market, towards the production and circulation of goods, and movement inwards, towards the accumulation and consumption of the products of work, corresponds symbolically to the opposition between the male body, self-enclosed and directed towards the outside world, and the female body, resembling the dark, damp house, full of food, utensils and children . . . (1977: 92)

The monolithic status of such biologically generated divisions of male and female as these translate into categories of in and out, public and private, has been widely challenged. Similar oppositions are quite differently aligned, for example, in East Asian spatial organization, as Roxanna Waterson has clearly shown (1990: 170); she points out the falsely unitary nature of Bourdieu's analysis, the problems and limitations that face the male ethnographer in his search for information about women's perception of space (197), and so calls attention to the role of the cultural cartographer in creating a map of the body.

Given such physical and intimate dimensions of the construction of the place/self dynamic, the logical sequitur for Tuan then becomes defining "how space and the experience of spaciousness are related to the human sense of competence and of freedom" (1977: 50). But this progression also brings up problems of restriction and confinement, the issue of the social production of space, and its connection to power; as Foucault reminds us, "space is fundamental in any exercise of power" (1984: 252). When place dictates or confines self, the critical focus switches to the underpinning ideologies that govern place and space. Analyses of environment stripped of its relation to a subject describe an estranged aesthetic, where space and place, and the individual's relation to them, can be objectified, commercialized, and exploited. A landscape, as Raymond Williams and many others after him have demonstrated, may give visual, aesthetic, and palpable form to political ideology; the built landscape of the eighteenth-century English park, for example, displays power and pride of ownership, while the ideology of its representation in landscape art serves "to naturalise, and hence to mystify, basic property relations" (Daniels and Cosgrove, 1988: 7).

The relationship of the individual to the state is enacted through space, which itself functions as a "supremely mediatory concept" (Jameson, 1990: 125), and the decentered theoretical viewpoint and the centered viewpoint of the subject may be successfully mediated by what Nicholas Entrikin calls the "betweenness of place" (1991: 5). This fluctuating quality is a great benefit in Fredric Jameson's view, because it "makes it impossible for us to evoke the aesthetic without at once beginning to slip into the cognitive on the one hand, and the sociopolitical on the other" (125). Rather, it obliges us to try to negotiate between them.

To bring these arguments a little closer to medieval Iceland, we can ask how Grettir, a legal outlaw and social outcast who is continually displaced, might stand in relation to the land. To what extent does land serve as an agent for legal or territorial directives, or serve as the space within which Grettir creates or imposes self? How can we approach the idea of the aesthetic that is implied by Gunnar's refusal to leave the land he loves and finds so beautiful? What are the ideologies of power that Gudrun enacts, reinforces, or resists in her choices to move or stay put? My discussion of Gudrun's situation will highlight another important dimension of the place/self dynamic. Freedom to move, to change one's place and hence control one's relationship to space, are legal and physical freedoms, inevitably bound up with gendered social practices, and to ask what is the specific relation of the female self to place is to involve and question these practices.

Women's relation to place is only now beginning to be explored. Recent studies have focused on the American frontier experience,[4] and it is
fascinating, though speculative, to ask some of the same questions about
Icelandic women's experience of settlement of a "wilderness" far more
challenging in that resources were more limited and habitable land more
scarce. Annette Kolodny (1984: 4) argues that the North American continent becomes "psychosexualized" by men as a virginal fantasy in which
varieties of aggression and domination are played out, and her question
then becomes how women "find a place" on this masculine cultural
map. Early American narratives written by women suggest that they experience wilderness via existing cultural and religious metaphors (Kolodny, 1984: 28), but we have no such direct evidence for the experience
of Icelandic women. What evidence we do have suggests that there were
relatively few women—at least those who may be named and identified—involved in the Icelandic frontier experience: "The commonplace
that frontiers attract men disproportionately" (Clover, 1990: 120) was
true of Iceland.[5] For information on how these medieval women might
have experienced their "new world" we have to turn again to the sagas
and keep asking different kinds of questions of them.

Although there is no developed body of research on the subject of
women's connection to place, recent feminist, ecofeminist, and ecological critical thinking share a preoccupation with rethinking self/other
divisions as these are imposed on or derived from place. The premise of
interrelatedness, that everything has an effect on everything else in our
biosphere, has long been a fundamental tenet of ecocriticism; we exist
within a network of biosocial relationships that define and sustain us. To
isolate self from its environment, or to promote or aggrandize self at the
expense of environment, is to ignore, at our own peril, the balance and
harmony of this network. Feminist critics and psychologists have argued
for the necessity of the female self's redefinition with regard to a historically masculinized Other, and have asserted a female psychology of self
based on connection and constituted by interrelationship, in contradis-
tinction to masculine definitions of self constituted by separation and
isolation.

To draw the parallel is in many ways to simplify a complex and ongoing debate between ecology and feminism.[6] For example, ecofeminists
have seen masculine domination of women as analogous to masculine
domination and exploitation of earth's resources, and tend to be wary
of new directions in ecocriticism that challenge anthropomorphism
without first acknowledging and dismantling its underlying androcen-
trism. Despite the many points of disagreement, however, these critics

are concerned to revise and reconstitute the self/other relationship as it is determined by our connection to place. They acknowledge that place— our sense of place, of being in place, in harmony with place—is vital to our sense of self.

Contemporary critical laments concerning the impoverishment and alienation of the modern self, male or female, as it is displaced, estranged from place, contain the seeds of a return to Wordsworth and Dewey's notions of aesthetic harmony and unity. "Most of us have lost," Gregory Bateson asserts, "that sense of unity of biosphere and humanity which would bind and reassure us all with an affirmation of beauty" (1979: 17). One of the problems inherent in this return to unity has always been that it is very hard to talk about it, to describe or analyze it in terms of an ongoing relationship of place and self. Mystery and religion—not to mention the problems of nostalgia, privileging of the subject, and the delusion of origins—intervene, and none of these helps, at least not initially, to bring us closer to hypothesizing the medieval Icelander's relation to place.

Iceland and Icelanders

How can we describe division or continuum of self and place in medieval Iceland? In order to locate these "places" and identify these "selves" that I have been discussing theoretically, I turn now to a more specific consideration of the relationship of a people to their land. The history of the settlement and development of the Icelandic Freestate (930–1262 A.D.), the setting for the majority of the sagas, is complex and far beyond the scope of my present study, but some key concepts that characterize the Icelanders' relationship to their land can be isolated. Kirsten Hastrup believes this relationship to be unique. In her wide-ranging anthropological study of medieval Iceland, she argues that Icelanders created "a separate reality" and inhabited an "autonomous semantic space," which came to an end with the Icelanders' submission to Norway in 1262 (1985: 204). Unique or not, the Icelanders' conceptualizations of space and place and their connections to them are highly individualized and sometimes deeply contradictory.

To begin with, isolating a self/place dynamic may represent an arbitrary kind of carving up of the spectrum of Icelandic experience. Hastrup suggests that "time, space, quality, society, and individuals seem to coalesce" (68) in the Icelandic notion of *veröld* (world), which combines *verr* (man) with *öld* (age, epoch). Interestingly, Icelandic bigamy laws provide one of the most concrete realizations of this close conceptualization of time and space. Bigamy was illegal in Iceland, but in changing places and going to Norway—in moving to another place and hence another time— a man could legally marry a second time (Hastrup, 1985: 91). Hastrup contends that "measuring the world in Iceland was a matter of collating temporal, spatial, and social realities" (61); the self's relation to place is thus mediated by crisscrossings and intersections of varieties of experience that are arguably peculiarly Icelandic, and in many cases peculiar to the terrain of Iceland.

Of Hastrup's many examples, I have chosen just a few. Conceptions of time, for instance, were much connected to social and legal realities: the sun designation "shaft-high" was considered a time description of legal standing (1985: 23); naming of Icelandic months paralleled social and economic factors (*egg-tið*, "egg-time," was the name for the second month of summer; 33). Place-names are invested with meaning in space and time, as in Breidafjord ("Broadfjord") or Vapnafjord ("Weaponfjord"), and farm names and locations become identified with the people who live there. Especially interesting to me in my attempt to describe a place/self dynamic is Hastrup's assertion that "movements rather than static indications are of prime significance in conceptualization of space" (52). North and west are directional goals, and topographical features can reorient directions (54). The traveler's direction is described in terms of the ultimate goal of the journey; "direction as goal" becomes part of the "semantic load" of a given term (55). One does not travel in a straight line in Iceland, and the nature of the terrain makes kilometers a highly ineffective means of measurement; instead, horse-riding distances (*rastir*, "rests") were used as a conjunction of physical and conceptual measurement of space, though the travelers' orientation—where they were coming from and going to—was also included in the definition of distance. Moreover, topographical coastal features could also reorient directions: because of the mountainous terrain, traveling *to* the coast becomes associated with downward movement, and traveling *from* the coast is associated with upward movement (54).

Hastrup's descriptions of directionality made perfect sense of our experience of traveling in Iceland. Kilometers as measurements are not to be trusted, despite the (intermittent) existence of paved road. We became engaged in a lively discussion with one Icelander who insisted, with absolute and unshakable certainty, that a stretch of road we had driven the previous day was about thirty kilometers, only five or so of which were paved. Marijane had been driving while I pored over a variety of maps, and from our different vantage points we were both convinced that we had traveled between fifty-five and sixty kilometers. We very nearly ran out of gas on that road, the result of a combination of factors. As often happened, different nuances of meaning were to be gleaned from our maps, as well as from the available signposts, and from our interpretation of them. The weather was foul, and the road largely unpaved and dangerously slippery. We "measured" every kilometer mentally and emotionally, and—though I will still maintain that we were "right"—the unbridgeable and passionately maintained gap in our computations suggests that distance is indeed measured by experience, by the nature and difficulty of passage, and by the point of view of the traveler.

It is the relationship, the means of connection between points, that signifies, as opposed to the abstraction of the points themselves. But, and this for me becomes a peculiarly Icelandic paradox, the fluidity of relationship is finally contained within the literal and abstract boundaries of the socius. Where and how you understood yourself to be "in place" is, Hastrup argues, ultimately a social positioning, or rather a mapping of the self according to sociopolitical rather than geographical coordinates. "Ultimate orientation," Hastrup states, "was society-centred in contrast to the ego-centred model of proximate direction" (1985: 57), because ultimate direction was based on the sociopolitical and legal division of the country into quarters. Jesse Byock has suggested that the law encodes and embodies "cultural focus" in medieval Iceland (1988: 7), and this is a powerful, pervasive, and essentially nonabstract characterization. Hastrup shows how the idea of law and the presence of the lawspeaker govern conceptualizations of time and religion (47); indeed, the concepts of geographical place and the law merge completely in the Icelanders' single term for their land and their society—*vár lög* ("our law"; Hastrup, 1985: 121). The power of the socius, as this is mapped out or encoded in law, has a determining force in mapping both self and self in place.

This point raises many, if not contradictions, then certainly deep tensions between the elements that comprise the place/self dialectic. I shall explore these elements in my discussions of Gunnar, Gudrun, and Grettir. I return to the same kinds of questions that reconfigure categories of in and out, of social, legal, and spatial boundaries that govern self and place. Where is the self placed that is outside the law, or how does the self confined within the law claim its own place?

Moreover, the demands of the socius and the requirements of the law often conflict to produce a problematic relationship between the individual and the land. The Icelandic "frontier" settlers began with an already-complex relationship, which in turn was changed and further complicated by social and religious developments throughout the period (see Hastrup, 1985: 178–204). A central tension existed between the idea

Plate 1. "Beowulf's *beorg*" overlooking Weder Isle Fjord. Photo by Randolph Swearer.

Plate 2. Fagraskogafell, one of Grettir's hideouts.

Plate 3. Looking from Gudrun and Bolli's homesite over to Laugar.

Plate 4. Gudrun's gravestone at Helgafell.

Plate 5. Gódafoss.

Plate 6. Two weathers, one landscape: a familiar Icelandic scene.

Plate 7. Drangey with the Kerling (the "Old Woman").

Plate 8. Cliffs of Drangey.

Plate 9. Climbing Drangey.

Plate 10. Drangey Blade.

Plate 11. The ladder to the top of Drangey.

Plate 12. A glimpse of the grassy top of
Drangey.

Plate 13. Drangey from Reykir Point, Grettir's four-mile swim.

Plate 14. Ásta recovers from her valiant swim.

of individual ownership and the demands of the kin group, or *aett*. Early individual settlers laid claim to large tracts of land, but the concept of private ownership coexisted with claims of certain members of the kin group and of articles of law. Individual owners were in some measure perceived as holding the land in trust for their heirs, who had to be consulted in any decisions regarding its sale or use (189). Although the codification of this relationship, found in the Norwegian legal principle of *oðal*, was not spelled out specifically in Icelandic law, Hastrup believes that the early Icelanders retained a concept of kin ownership, which differed from that of the Norwegians in that the land in Iceland was newly claimed.

The individual "frontier" land-rush mentality coexisted with a strong code of communal responsibility, and this balance was often uneasy. A pastor in Midfjord (who helped us to find many saga sites and who is pictured in figure 18 next to a "Grettir stone") described to us a similar modern tension involving self and community as he spoke of his way of communicating with his parishioners individually and at local gatherings. When he first moved to the region, it had been hard for him to fulfill the part of his job that designated him as counselor and confidant; even talking to his parishioners had been difficult. Stories might be told of other people and places, from the past or the present, but people never told stories about themselves. The self, he said, was discrete, integral, not to be intruded upon—but equally there was a strong need to establish community, to connect the self with the group. After several years in the area, he was still struggling to identify the needs of individuals and to balance these with the demands of the community.

The migration of the first settlers to Iceland in the ninth century has been explained in several ways. Whether we imagine those settlers as land-grabbing pioneers, refugees deprived of their land who were fleeing the high-handed Norwegian king and his policies of land reform—Harald Fairhair refused to honor the principle of *oðal* and demanded land rent from communal property (Hastrup, 1985: 190)—or adventuresome Vikings, what they all held in common is simply summarized by Byock: "The task facing the newcomers was to create a society on an empty island with a limited habitable area" (1988: 2). The idea of the island as blank slate and the settlement as social experiment suggests, according to another critic, that "it was a country that ought to have been a Utopia. It had: no foreign policy, no defence forces, no king, no lords, no peasants, no dispossessed aborigines, no battles (till late on), no dangerous animals, and no very clear taxes. What, given this blank slate, could possibly go wrong? Why is their literature all about killing each other?" (Shippey, 1989: 17).

Indeed, a great deal of murder and retaliation is described in the sagas, which, whether or not one accords them any degree of historical veracity, are nevertheless extremely valuable as cultural documents, descriptive of certain kinds of cultural focus. The Icelandic sagas, Byock (1984–85: 167) further points out, are *not* about chivalric exploits or quests for any variety of Holy Grail, but are more concerned with domestic and agricultural issues such as marital disputes or disagreements over livestock, field boundaries, and property ownership. The violence has much to do with territoriality in its starkest, most unforgiving aspect—the seizure, settlement, and retention of land (whether by force or by marriage), the desire for ownership and domination.

In the context of this clear territorial imperative, to what extent is the landscape bound up with accession to and demonstration of identity, and how are ownership and identity connected? What does the idea of ownership connote to a group of scattered individuals who are claiming and naming often-hostile terrain, farming and surviving on the periphery of a vast and unforgiving wilderness that comprises the uninhabitable center of the country? The Icelanders' relation to the land is even now very much one of exterior to interior: the socialized margin interacts with and is conditioned by the spatial centrality of wilderness. This point was brought home to me when within a day of my arrival in Reykjavik I had heard from three completely unrelated sources detailed accounts of accidents and deaths that had just happened to families who were crossing the "interior." This had been a very bad year for deaths, I heard repeatedly. During my next visit, I read that that year had been particularly bad for accidents, but light on fatalities. The city dwellers on the margin keep an ongoing log of events in the uninhabited center.

The medieval Icelanders sought to codify and control their connection to the land, creating a highly sophisticated legal system that in turn seemed to produce an endless series of disputes over land in the sagas. Clearly the Icelandic relation to land involves more than a simple territorial imperative of violence and domination, and this is where the concept of geopiety becomes useful. Yi-Fu Tuan borrows the term from John K. Wright and develops its cosmic, religious, and mythological implications on a broad scale; what I am most concerned with here is the aspect of reciprocity invoked by the concept. As the elements of the compound suggest, geopiety involves a profound commitment and connection to, and passion for, place, or one's place on earth. Also implied is a respect for that place, a reverence that expresses devotion to the land but also a fear of its power over and power to define the individual. Such reverence acknowledges a power that must also be propitiated, whether in the form of sacrifice as in the Greek and classical traditions, or in the form of modern ecological consciousness. Both ancient and modern views point to the necessity of living in a reciprocal relationship to our chosen place on earth.

The concept of the sacred nature of home and land, of the homeland in classical antiquity, must be substantially revised in the context of medieval Iceland. Tuan quotes Isocrates' impassioned speech on behalf of Athens and points up the contrast nicely:

> We did not become dwellers in this land by driving others out of it, nor by finding it uninhabited, nor by coming together here a motley horde composed of many races; but we are of a lineage so noble and so pure that throughout our history we have continued in possession of the very land which gave us birth, since we are sprung from its very soil and are able to address our city by the names which we apply to our nearest kin; for we alone of all the Hellenes have the right to call our city at once nurse and fatherland and mother. (1976: 25)

The notion of the "sacred hearth," indeed the meaning of the idea of "home" itself, might be remade in the light of two general observations about Iceland and Icelandic culture. The first is the nature of the terrain, something that has changed relatively little since the time of the sagas. "Land of fire and ice" may sound like a tourist brochure (in fact, this phrase does come from a tourist brochure), but it accurately suggests the uncanny varieties of landscapes made possible by both volcanic and glacial activities. The landscape is eerie, stark, overwhelmingly beautiful, and overwhelming in its contrasts of beauty and unrelenting hostility, of reassuringly familiar fertile valleys and unimagined extraterrestrial vistas spewing smoke and sulphur. When I read in *Egil's Saga* of how Egil, the murderous Viking who started killing at the age of six, is wont to calm down when he returns home to Iceland, that he is content to farm his land and leave "most men in peace" (chapter 66), I wonder about the power of place. The larger-than-life characteristics of this most violent of Icelanders are subdued, perhaps balanced, by the exacting realities of his home. This Viking meets his match in his home.

What indeed might home be to a Viking? This leads to my second general observation about Icelandic culture, one peculiar to saga times: the cultural and political importance of the capacity to travel. Maritime historian G. J. Marcus argues that it was largely the Norse mastery of ship design that made possible the early Viking raids (1980: 39) and the settlement of Iceland: "It can hardly be overemphasized that the main and decisive factor in this great movement was the remarkable progress achieved during the eighth and ninth centuries in Norse shipbuilding, seamanship, and navigation" (49). Hastrup maintains that the converse is also true in that one of the factors leading to the decline of the Icelandic Freestate was the gradual erosion of the seafaring tradition (1985: 225). The capacity to travel, the tradition of travel, the political freedom to travel, all of which characterize the society of the sagas—how are these factors in defining that which is home?

In many different cultures, Tuan suggests, home and journey comprise one of the basic binary divisions where "the two elements correspond to the positive and negative poles" (1971: 188).

> The sense of nurturing, of rest, is strongly associated with "home." To live, one has to labour, work, and take risks in alien places. Home as refuge is the reverse of challenge and strain . . . To travel is to take risks, to be aware of inhospitable lands and circumstances; the experience of insecurity, by providing contrast, intensifies the identification of home with security and rest. (189)

But surely the connotations of negativity, of security and insecurity, must be commuted, or perhaps their relation to each other might be re-arranged, in the context of the medieval Icelander's experience.

Throughout the sagas, taking off periodically and traveling for years at a stretch is a standard choice for many men, young and old, and an occasional choice for women (see notes 12 and 13 of this chapter). Such behavior is accepted, praised, expected. One might even postulate travel as a distinct cultural value, both ethical and material, and, moreover, an intellectual necessity: "for a man is thought to grow ignorant if he doesn't ever travel beyond this country of Iceland" (*Laxdæla Saga*, chapter 72). Home as a value might also be reexamined. The sacred hearth of classical antiquity might be transported in the form of clods of earth, which were buried in the new chosen homeland, as when the Carthaginians founded the new Rome (Tuan, 1976: 26). The Icelanders had a different method; the sagas describe the custom of the first settlers who when within sight of land would throw the wooden pillars of their high seat overboard. Consider this passage from *Laxdæla Saga*: "After that, Unn went round all the Breidafjord Dales and took possession of as much land as she pleased. Then she sailed right up to the head of the fjord, and there her high-seat pillars had been washed ashore. She now thought it had been clearly shown where she should build her home" (chapter 5). In this instance, home and journey define each other; or, more precisely, home is a function of journey. The land chooses Unn, even as she lays claim to it, and we are faced with the entanglement of the simpler directive of territorial domination and the more complex reciprocity of geopiety. Consider also a gruesome alternative version of this process that entangles the dead with the living. Egil's grandfather, Kveldulf, dies on his way to Iceland, but insists that he will take land there nonetheless; he orders his coffin to be thrown overboard to mark out where his son's homestead should be built (*Egil's Saga*, chapter 27).

Tuan also points out that, like all binary structures, home and journey will define each other in relationship and in context. With this in mind I return to the dynamic of place and self. As I predicted, the boundaries of these two elements have become blurred, and I take up my initial plan of discussing first "places" and then "selves" advisedly, and mainly for the convenience of linear organization.

Places in Question

I began work on this section with several hundred slides of specific places, images evoking literal places and literary questions, stopping places along the path of a mental and physical journey. I have chosen to focus on about a dozen images, some of which are mine and others Collingwood's, and to regard these as visual prisms that reflect, evoke, and contribute to our ongoing series of questions about the nature of place, and the layers of negotiative activities that places create and represent.

Skallagrim's Grave near Borg (Figure 8)

I begin here simply because this is one of my favorite images. Skallagrim was Kveldulf's son and father of Egil, the hero of *Egil's Saga*. Father and son did not get along particularly well; each tried to kill the other on several occasions, and the two of them fought frequently over money. The saga tells us:

> Egil had a burial mound raised there on the tip of the headland, and inside it Skallagrim was laid with his horse, weapons, and blacksmith's tools. There's no mention of any money being placed in the mound with him. (Chapter 58)

Three sets of local inhabitants of modern Borgarnes gave directions to this unmarked mound in the local cemetery, overhung with laundry, insisting that it was "the" grave, and we had had enough experience of

Figure 8. Skallagrim's grave near Borg (with laundry).

the Icelanders' accurate knowledge of both their literary and historical pasts to accept this as true.

This gravesite was more the rule than the exception, in that there are few modern markers or signposts to the past in Iceland. According to David Lowenthal, such markers "induce an academic frame of mind" and "make us consider function more than appearance, structure rather than impression" (1979: 110–11). Moreover, "because signs inevitably classify what they identify, they also encourage us to compare historical sights . . . Signposts reduce historical experience from environmental flux to the kind of order found in history books; they make the visible past feel more like the written record" (111). This unmarked place marks out a piece of literary and historical reality that is experienced, re-created in the visual present.

Markar River and Hlidarend (Figures 9 and 10)

In *Njal's Saga* there is a powerful literary representation of the power of place, a possible instance of Tuan's idea of "geopiety." When the relatively mild-mannered and law-abiding Gunnar Hamundarson, close friend of Njal the lawgiver, is finally provoked to violence, he receives a sentence of temporary outlawry at the Althing for his killing of Thorgeir Otkelsson. He accepts the decree (his life being forfeit as an outlaw otherwise), readies his ship to leave Iceland, and says his good-byes. The saga reports:

> They rode down to the Markar River. Just then Gunnar's horse stumbled, and he had to leap from the saddle. He happened to glance up towards his home and the slopes of Hlidarend. "How lovely the slopes are," he said, "more lovely than they have ever seemed to me before, golden cornfields and new-mown hay. I am going back home and I will not go away." (Chapter 75)

His choice has important consequences, as we shall see in my discussion of this same situation from the point of view of "self," but here I want to consider the power of place and its connection to the non-medieval onlooker. Figures 9 and 10 show the icy-gray Markar River and the fertile slopes of Gunnar's home. This *is* one of the most fertile and lush areas of Iceland, although I found no luxuriant cornfields, and the day when I took my photographs, as you might be able to see, was one of the dreariest, dampest, and darkest of the trip. It crossed my mind that had I been Gunnar on that day, I might have pressed on to the ship. Collingwood, however, agrees rhapsodically with Gunnar, while trying to account for, or possibly apologize for, his own subjectivity. His diary account of his own trip reads as follows:

> In the morning we learned once more that scenery and romance are inseparable. Gunnar's home, which he so passionately loved, was worthy of his affection—even from the sentimental view of the landscapist. He may not have known why he "thought it so fair": perhaps the blake acres commended themselves to him as much for practical farming as for poetical fancy. But no modern traveller can fail to note that the one place of all the world where a man, in those rude and distant days, chose deliberately to die, rather than to go

Figure 9. Markar River.

Figure 10. Gunnar's homesite at Hlidarend.

out into exile from it, was so magnificently situated. (Collingwood and Stefánsson, 1899: 30)

The weather was a factor for us even as it might have been for Gunnar. Icelanders experienced unusually mild and relatively benign climatic conditions during the period 870–1170 (Byock, 1988: 80). I stretch the connection—the sagas were written down a century or so later—in order to stress the idea of connection. Collingwood calls my attention to his own activity of structuring and valuing place as he interprets Gunnar's actions, and reminds me both that what connects Gunnar, saga writer, Collingwood, and myself *is* this place, and that literary, historical, and geographical realities intersect in the experience of place.

My remaining sites are from *Laxdæla Saga*, where the saga writer's knowledge of local landscape often proved to be accurate to the most minute detail. Each place, or piece of landscape, raises the same kinds of questions invited by the possibility of such close literary, historical, and geographical parallelism.

Two Views of Our Candidate for "Kjartan's Stone" in Svinadale (Figures 11 and 12)

Kjartan is ambushed by Bolli, his close childhood friend who has married Gudrun, whom Kjartan also loves. The situation is tense. In a frenzy of vengeance, presumably brought on because Gudrun really wanted to marry Kjartan but he did not claim her hand quickly enough, Gudrun has persuaded Bolli to ambush Kjartan with a band of men. The saga states (I'm piecing together here from chapter 48–49):

> They rode over to Svinadale, and dismounted beside a ravine called Hafragill. There they tethered their horses and sat down to wait. Bolli was silent all day, and lay on the brink above the ravine . . . Kjartan and his companions came up quickly for they were riding hard, and when they had passed south of the ravine they caught sight of the ambush and recognized the men. Kjartan jumped off his horse at once and turned to face the Osvifssons. There was a huge boulder standing nearby, and there Kjartan said they would make their stand.

Kjartan dies at Bolli's hand. The site is described in the saga, and marked on a modern map as "Kjartan's Stone," but, predictably, there are no signposts or modern markers at the site itself. After many hours of

Figures 11 and 12. Two views of our candidate for "Kjartan's Stone" in Svinadale.

Figure 13. Graveyard and church at Borg.

exploring the gills and contours of Svinadale, traveling up and down the valley three or four times, and locating only one suitable boulder, we were ready to conclude that this, indeed, *might* be "the very place . . . "

Graveyard and Church at Borg (Figure 13)

The saga tells us that Kjartan was buried by his uncle in the churchyard at Borg, former home of the poet-Viking Egil:

> Thorstein Egilsson had had a church built at Borg. He took Kjartan's body home with him, and Kjartan was buried at Borg. The church had only recently been consecrated, and was still hung with white. (*Laxdæla Saga*, chapter 51)

Collingwood had painted the gravesite, in his day marked with a gravestone. He writes: "In the churchyard is the grave of Kjartan, so named by an ancient tradition confirmed by the runic stone that lies on it, the only one in Iceland: bearing words carved by some medieval hand . . . Here sleeps the hero, Kjartan, son of Olaf" (59). As it turns out, Collingwood was wrong. The runestone, now moved to the National Museum of Iceland, is dated from the fourteenth century, and the cryptic runic

Figure 14. The *tun-brekka* at Hoskuldstead.

inscription has been reinterpreted to suggest a quite different name. My disappointment upon discovering this at the museum in Reykjavik was profound. The signpost, the marker, had pointed in a different direction. Was this, then, "the very place"? And how multiple and subject to revision were my ways of knowing whether it was or not?

The *tun-brekka* at Hoskuldstead (Figure 14)

Kjartan's grandfather, Hoskuld, buys a beautiful concubine at a slave market on his travels in Norway—an entirely legal operation, apparently (Karras, 1988: 73)—and brings her home, much to the consternation of his wife in Iceland. The concubine, who is presumed deaf and dumb, has a son, Olaf, by Hoskuld, to the further consternation of his wife. The saga states:

It so happened one morning that Hoskuld was out of doors seeing to his farm; it was a fine day, and the dawn sun was shining. He heard the sound of voices and went over to the stream at the foot of the sloping homefield. There he saw two people he knew well: it was his son Olaf, and the boy's mother. He realized then that she was not speechless at all, for she was talking busily to the child. Hoskuld now went over to them and asked her what her name was, and told her there was no point in concealing it any longer. She agreed, and they sat down on the slope of the homefield. Then she said, "If you want to know my name, I am called Melkorka." Hoskuld asked her to tell him more about her family. "My father is called Myrkjartan, and he is a king in Ireland," she said. "I was taken captive and enslaved when I was fifteen." (*Laxdæla Saga,* chapter 13)

Figure 14 is an image of "a" (if not "the") *tun-brekka,* the specific Icelandic term used in the saga for this piece of landscape, a sloping homefield, where Melkorka's Cinderella story unfolds. Differing only slightly from the position of slave, the actual social and legal status of the concubine and her children contrasts rather bleakly with Melkorka's story (Karras, 1988: 75); her tale of female enfranchisement via lineage and her bold claiming of her own history and language as she teaches the child her native language of Irish, are the stuff of, if not fantasy, then certainly romance. This site, then, is the "real" location of a variety of unlikely, or "unreal," social possibilities. My photograph of this place matches almost exactly Collingwood's painting of a century previous, but with what kind of exactitude do either of us approach or re-create the moment, the place of a thousand years ago?

I come squarely up against the problems of unitary definitions of place illustrated by Tuan's analogy of the "Eureka impulse" that "good" humanist scholars can so rarely gratify because the very unity of the question "What is the nature of place?" becomes immediately and diversely particularized (Tuan, 1983: 70). Impossible though it may be to realize, I must acknowledge the extent to which such an impulse underlies and is embodied by the search for "the very place," particularly strongly present in these last images from *Laxdæla Saga.* To reiterate a point we wanted to make clear in our Introduction, however, the excitement of exactitude, of replication, is of course a variant on the search for origins, and, as such, partakes of nostalgia and closure of meaning, not to mention illusion.

Well of course it's an illusion. The illusion of belief, of certitude, was clearly brought home to me by a student's remark: "If I can say that I am standing on the very spot where Olaf the Peacock kills the ghost of Killer-Hrapp, what is it that I know? What am I saying that I believe?" A similar question is raised by the precise physical presence of the *tunbrekka* and the reality of Melkorka's Cinderella story.

In both cases the question "What is the nature of place?" and the answer begin to decompose, to splinter into a myriad of further considerations. To suggest, however, that the saga writer, Collingwood, and I have shared a point, or rather, a "place," of meaning is not to state that we have all fixed the "same" point, or defined the nature of this or that place. To claim this degree of identity brings us back to the problem of the mysterious point of unity between observer and observed: namely, that it is very hard to talk about it, to describe or analyze it in terms of an ongoing relationship of place and self. More accessible is the idea that the experience of place is a shared form of meaning, more obviously an experience, more readily and indeed appropriately apprehended as a process rather than stasis. Our three viewpoints converge in an experience of place, an experience of others' constructions of place in conjunction with one's own, of present negotiation with the past. These images of places, whether or not they are "the very places," might then frame a kind of functional and dynamic interdisciplinarity, or a prism of semiotic convergence. They frame a newly created space where the literary, the historical, and the cultural are in ongoing negotiation with the geographical, the personal, and the material—a place where the writing of the saga inevitably continues.

Selves in Place

Gunnar Hamundarson

I return to Gunnar of Hlidarend, designated as the "archetypal land-lover" by one of the foremost historians of the Viking period (Jones, 1984: 464), to ask some more questions about his individual perception. The image of law-abiding, peace-loving Gunnar as a working farmer, a landowner who is out doing manual labor in his own fields, is a realistic one: the "typical Icelandic householder" was by no means a "man of leisure" (Karras, 1988: 80). Gunnar is unusual perhaps in that despite ample provocation he is extremely slow to anger and loath to take vengeance. Interestingly, he is also self-conscious about his nonviolence. "But I wish I knew," he confides to his brother, "whether I am any the less manly than other men, for being so much more reluctant to kill than other men are" (*Njal's Saga,* chapter 54). He scrupulously stays within the bounds of the law, and even when it permits vengeance, he seeks other solutions to feuds. Finally he is provoked to violence, and he receives a sentence of temporary outlawry for a period of three years. The institution of outlawry was an important aspect of Iceland's relatively progressive social structure. "Dependence on outlawry," Byock explains, "exempted Iceland from the need to maintain a policing body to oversee the imposition of corporal punishment, execution, or incarceration" (1988: 29).

Outlawry, whether full or temporary, also involved confiscation of property.

Law-abiding Gunnar initially accepts the sentence, and assures Njal that "he had no intention of breaking his pledges" (chapter 74). On the way to his ship, however, he changes his mind. As his horse happens to stumble, he happens to look up, is struck by the beauty of his homeland, and decides to stay (see previous section of this chapter for a more detailed account). Gunnar's behavior, in fact, might be quite unsurprising and precedented in that he may have interpreted his fall as a traditional bad omen for travel, as did Erik the Red when, after his horse stumbled, he categorically declined to set out for Greenland (*Grænlendinga Saga*, chapter 3). The accidental or formulaic elements in this first situation are overlaid by Gunnar's equally deliberate refusal to leave his home a second time, when his friend Olaf the Peacock has offered sanctuary to him and his wife. Gunnar thinks about the proposition and is temporarily tempted, "but when the time came, he did not care to go" (*Njal's Saga*, chapter 75). Gunnar receives full outlawry for his second refusal to leave. In his decision to stay, nonetheless, Gunnar is not only defying the laws he had struggled to uphold, he is also effectively choosing to die. Not only could an outlaw be killed with impunity, but the wise and prescient Njal has foretold Gunnar's death if, having killed twice in the same family, he risks breaking the settlement (chapter 73). Yet Gunnar will not leave his home, his land. Why?

This is one of the few places in the sagas where landscape is identified as aesthetically beautiful, but the aesthetic argument raises more questions than it answers. I have already recounted my own disappointed reaction in contrast to Collingwood's delighted appreciation of the same scene; defining Gunnar's aesthetic sense is equally problematic. In his controversial book *The Saga Mind*, M. I. Steblin-Kamenskii asserts that aesthetic perception of nature simply did not exist in the world of the sagas, because this would imply an opposition of nature to "man" and the differentiation of nature as an object external to human consciousness (1973: 77). Distinctions between truth and art, the historical and the artistic, the human and the natural, self and place, only become articulated by self-consciousness in language, and Steblin-Kamenskii argues that the syncretism of the saga world and mind makes no such distinctions.

Such syncretism finds parallels elsewhere in the medieval world. Distinguishing a self, a perceiving subject, is a problem in medieval journey narratives, as Mary Campbell suggests. There is no place for the "I" voice in early travel literature through which we might gain an understanding of perceptions of place; although self "becomes necessary as a rhetorical presence" (1988: 15), it functions to translate the topography of the journey into a "series of incidents rather than a series of landscapes and objects" (29). Campbell's remarks echo a familiar commentary on saga style, i.e., that it focuses on narration of events rather than their psychological import, and consequently our reconstruction of the "I" will necessarily be heavily mediated.

This apparent syncretism has both advantages and drawbacks; there may be no "I" voice in the sagas but "the lack of consciousness of authorship is the lack of consciousness of the limits of human personality" (Steblin-Kamenskii, 1973: 51). Steblin-Kamenskii does contend, somewhat mysteriously, that the "human personality was less distinct in people's minds" (65). The lack of differentiation makes both sides of the dialectic harder to imagine. This collapsibility of categories is reminiscent of Hastrup's arguments for cross-conceptualization in medieval Iceland, and although I might disagree with Steblin-Kamenskii's conflation of internal and external, it obliges us to locate the self/place relationship culturally, to contextualize the concept of the aesthetic, and our reconstruction of it.

Notwithstanding this relative aesthetic—the relative beauty of the land and the equally relative eye of the past or present beholder—Gunnar's behavior is difficult to explain. His decision is profoundly irrational in that it ignores the code that gave meaning to his previous actions, but if we understand it as an expression of passion, of Tuan's "geopiety," what gods is Gunnar propitiating here? His sacrifice is his own life. We might also label this instance of geopiety self-destructive and stubborn territoriality, an assertion of possession, of ownership. The reciprocal aspect of Gunnar's geopious gesture is curiously internalized; his "gods" are within. In staying, Gunnar asserts, perhaps defines, self, discovers identity, and simultaneously sacrifices both. Gunnar's conflict also places the natural aesthetic, which might be hypothesized if not defined, in familiar opposition to social and legal imperatives, severing the connection to the natural by legislating the cultural, dividing the geopious impulse from its social context. Gunnar may not live in peace in his home, refuse violent action, obey the law, *and* farm his land at the same time. Perhaps his choice shows the irrationality of the impossibility of these apparently reasonable demands. The power of place is pitted against the power of the socius, but the victory of place demands the sacrifice, entirely voluntary in Gunnar's case, of the individual's life.

Grettir Asmundarson

Tolerant, law-abiding, and on the whole amiable, Gunnar stands in contrast to the outlaw/hero of *Grettir's Saga*. Grettir is not interested in peaceful coexistence or lawful behavior; he embraces violence and is not fond of any kind of work, farming or otherwise. Yet Grettir's career as an outlaw writes large the issues that Gunnar's individual quandary raises in particular and miniature detail. The single instance of connection to place begs the larger social questions that Grettir's roving progress throughout Iceland insistently dramatizes but does not finally answer. In fact, Grettir problematizes the self/place dialectic that I have been trying to outline to an extent that obliges me to rethink the terms of its oppositions. Grettir is a study in contradiction, ambiguity, perversity, and, ultimately, uncontainability. As a hero, he elicits mixed responses from his audiences within and without the saga, and I shall examine my own deeply ambivalent fascination with the contradictions he embodies when I take "the road to Drangey" in the final chapter of this book. Here I want to look at some of the ways in which he might reconfigure or reconstitute the individual's connection to place.

Grettir is a notoriously unpleasant and belligerent child who is cruel to animals (horses and geese, admittedly, rather than the more cuddly kind). He is not so much lazy as disinclined to work, especially at the bidding of others, despite his tremendous physical strength; he is a poor talker, but a fair poet, fond of riddling and, by extension, of disguise and magic; he is fabulously strong and pitifully unlucky. He saves the day and kills monsters (superhuman beings) in more standard heroic fashion, but often is gratuitously violent, lacks self-control, dislikes being alone, and—a fact that is curiously validating, exonerating, and endearing—is afraid of the dark. He slays the monster Glam, but this piece of heroism is also the hero's undoing, because before he dies Glam predicts that Grettir will be haunted by the monster's eyes, and that he will dread being alone as a result (*Grettir's Saga*, chapter 35).

The antisocial temperament that fears solitude, the social and legal outcast attempting, literally, to find a place to be, the struggle to maintain self or simply to stay alive, the exile who will not leave—these are some of the elements of Grettir's situation that challenge the very foundations of the social contract in medieval Iceland. Unlike Gunnar, Grettir does not declare why he refuses to leave. When he returns from his Norwegian travels—the requisite Viking roving—Grettir has been declared an outlaw and is already deeply involved in family vengeance feuds, one sanctioned "arm" of the law that took the place of war (Byock,

1988: 109), and he does not appear even to consider obeying the law of outlawry. As he becomes progressively more enmeshed in various vengeance cycles interspersed with characteristic exploits and displays of strength, he is always on the move; often rejected and occasionally aided by Icelanders whose legal duty it is to shun him, he is always seeking a place to be: " 'These things are beyond my control,' said Grettir. *'And I have to be somewhere'* " (chapter 52, my emphasis).[7]

The many contradictions embodied by Grettir challenge the rule of law; the hero/outlaw figure insistently raises the questions of how to deal with his uncontainability when there is no social principle of incarceration, and how to eradicate the threat, the social evil, that he represents when there is no social principle of execution (other than the sanctioned killing of outlaws).[8] When we recall that law is inseparable from concepts of society, land, and country, we extend Grettir's challenge to the personal and political alignment of self and place. Grettir finally claims a place, quite to his liking, *outside* Iceland—stark, inaccessible, remote Drang Isle (see plates 7–12). He shares the island not only with his brother and a slave, but with exiled evil forces. Early priests sanctified only a portion of the island, relegating the northeastern part as an "abode of evil" (Swaney, 1991: 191); even today Icelanders will bless themselves before entering this area. Evil, too, has to *be* somewhere, apparently, and although Grettir comes "home" to Drangey in one sense, he nevertheless spends the greater part of his life as an outlaw moving from the socialized margin of the country further into the interior, the uninhabitable center of Iceland.

Grettir turns the inside out, the outside in, and confuses the boundaries of both; through force of personality and presence, he inhabits and brings into focus the *óbyggth,* "the 'uninhabited' space of the island, which was not defined other than by the negative criterion that it was not lived in" (Hastrup, 1985: 144). Hastrup develops the idea of negative definition in her discussion of outlawry; the compound concept of *vár lög* (as law/land, country/society) dictates that that which is "outside" the law, literally and legally, is the opposite and the negative of the "social," i.e., the "wild." This division of inside/outside permeates social and legal conceptions of space, beginning at the microlevel of domestic spatial arrangements and extending, according to Hastrup, to Icelandic cosmological geography (60).[9] "Outside the fence" (*útangarðs*), or beyond the periphery of the central farmhouse, the terrain of the nonsocial and antisocial unfolds in legally gradable degrees until the *óbyggth* takes over. The outlaw Grettir shares this negative space with a variety of supernatural beings (trolls, giants, elves) and others on the outs, as it were, with society, or without social identity, such as runaway slaves. One might place women here, too, though at the more social edge of this spatial spectrum. If "slavespace" is negative, in that slaves' legal rights as individuals either disappear or are extremely restricted under the law (see Karras, 1988: 96–121), then "womanspace" is peripheral, on the edge: sons inherited the central farmhouse, and women inherited the "outlying lands" (*útjarðir*; Hastrup, 191).

If the space Grettir inhabits is negative, does he define it, and if so, how? When Grettir hides out in Fagraskogafell (see plate 2), he finds a vantage lookout point that he literally inhabits. Helen Damico describes and interprets his actions thus:

> There is a hole right through the mountain that commands a view of the main path below, and it is that bore hole that Grettir inhabits. The image is one which presents the hero as integral to his environment, for he completes it. He fills nature's vacuum.
>
> Yet, characteristically, Grettir's actions are antithetical to that idea and his creative energy goes to masking the union. He constructs an illusion of empty space by placing across the entrance of the bore hole a piece of gray "homespun cloth." In so doing, he negates his existence. In essence, this is the nature of Grettir's psychic state during his nineteen years of exile—he must be willing to negate his identity. (1986: 8).

As part of this continual process of negation, and in keeping with Grettir's consistent role of spoiler, or at least producer of contradiction, Damico also calls attention to Grettir's repeated but failed attempts to "civilize the wasteland" (10) and to the antisocial identity within which she suggests Grettir is finally imprisoned, personally and geographically, on Drangey (11).

Damico raises several interesting issues that I want to examine. One is an implication that the "social" gives definition to the "wild," that Grettir cannot claim identity within the *óbyggth,* and the other is the primarily symbolic notion of the function of landscape in this saga. In a sense these two ideas reinforce each other. Places serve as a backdrop; they are seen as motifs, clues to or enhancers of the plot/text. *Grettir's Saga,* Damico argues, is highly unusual among the sagas in that it enables "symbolic articulation of dramatic action" (2); landscapes are thus rendered as socially ordered representations and the power of place allegorized and distanced. Although the symbolic values of landscape are part of a well-established traditional critical discussion of epic, heroic, and oral-formulaic literatures,[10] such ordering and distancing via allegorization can also diminish the actual power and presence of place. Or, rather, the symbolic mode may not be able to register the variables of presence.

Consider here the "reality" of Thorisdal, the hidden valley near a glacier, teeming with fat sheep and lush grass, that Grettir discovers and hides out in for a brief period. Whether or not this place exists has been much debated: "Readers must decide for themselves how far the author believed in Thorisdal as a real valley. Various expeditions have claimed success in their search for it, but they do not seem to have all arrived in the same place" (Hight, 1914: 244, note 164). This utopian, idyllic environment has also been designated the so-called locus amoenus of the saga in terms of symbolic landscape criticism (Damico, 3). When we went looking for this valley, we were impeded by weather, the condition of the secondary roads, the inadequacy of our rented vehicle (although I have trouble imagining the kind of machine that could have negotiated this terrain), and our general faintheartedness occasioned by all of the above.

What we did find later on, however, was an analogy, another magical valley in a different place and context. In southeast Iceland, coming to the end of a long day's drive, we turned off the main road and arrived at a small farmhouse tucked neatly at the foot of the massive Vatnajokull (the third largest glacier in the world). We believed we had previously arranged lodging here when still in Reykjavik. No, the pastor and his wife had no notification that we were coming; no, they no longer rented rooms out, they were getting too old for all that. Nonetheless, since we had showed up, they did have two immaculate rooms ready, and we were made very welcome. The couple was leaving, they told us, moving to Reykjavik to be with their children. I had assumed that life would be easier for them in the city; the looming gray presence of the glacier, flinty and forbidding in the evening sunlight, seemed to epitomize the challenges and hardships of the Icelandic winter, and the potentially alienating force of landscape. I was completely wrong. They maintained that they lived in a kind of benign microclimate facilitated by the proximity of the glacier. It was warmer, it rarely snowed, their livestock and their garden thrived; in fact, these two elderly people were most unenthusiastic about moving to the city and abandoning this magical niche. But Grettir, typically a man of contradiction, is quite ready to leave his magical valley, real or not, because he finds it too dull (chapter 61).

Desirable or not, fictional or otherwise, such places are certainly imaginable, and they exist on a variety of levels. In her anthropological fieldwork, Hastrup (1986) discovered an ongoing belief in "hidden valleys of plenty"; Grettir's idyllic situation retains a mythic currency and fascination, an imaginative outlet for displacing problems of existing social reality. If I remain on a literal rather than a mythic or literary level, however, once again the present "facts" of place—its power, presence, and reality—intervene in my theoretical dialogue. If I am to include them, I must return to two rather obvious observations. First, in Iceland the center is the margin; the edge of the wilderness, the social and geographical frontier, is contained within the island. The particular nature of the terrain gives a physical centrality to the "wild," one that can condition and possibly intervene in the symbolic order of the socialized margin. To start with, things are inside out, as it were, a reversal that is curiously imaged by the distinctively Icelandic term for permanent outlawry, *skóggangr*, "forest-going." The Norwegian term *útlagi*, outlaw, existed in the shared language of Old Norse; that the Icelanders chose to add a different term suggests to Hastrup that "Icelandic usages must have established themselves as particular realizations of a common concept" (1985: 140). Though dense and vast forests were and are plentiful in Norway, however, they did not and do not exist in Iceland. Early settlers cleared the bulk of existing woods, but these would always have been sparse (Hastrup, 1985: 139), and the term evokes less the idea of a dense forest that will veil and protect than a connotation of wilderness, nonsociety, the "wild." This idea of forest-going turns inward, recalling Gaston Bachelard's description of the "inner immensity" conjured by the forest, its evocation of a potential and infinite world of veiled space: "We do not have to be in the woods for long to experience the always rather anxious impression of 'going deeper and deeper' into a limitless world" (1969: 185). Although the "wild" center is bounded, limited by the socialized margin, Grettir enters a place and state of mind where the forest becomes a vast open tract of geographically, psychologically, and culturally uncharted territory. The outside turns in.

Second, the benign and nurturing landscape of Thorisdal notwithstanding, the places that the outlaw Grettir must inhabit, even the less remote places to which we managed to gain access, seem, perhaps more so to the modern observer, breathtakingly harsh, overwhelmingly difficult, a supreme challenge to human survival. These places are frightening in their power and beauty. Yet Grettir survives. This is the one aspect of his heroic personality that Marijane and I can thoroughly agree on and find compelling. The "fact" of these places juxtaposed to the "fact" that Grettir stays alive in them does not add up to the notion of negative identity. Here the forces and powers of self match those of place.

These places seem to be all prospect and no refuge, to recall one of the animal behaviorist approaches to the study of place, where we define our

Figure 15. Looking out to Drangey from Hegranes.

relation to place in terms of our perception of its level of hospitality to our survival and comfort, where we discover a balance between exploring and escaping that will define our place, and our self in relation to it. Or perhaps these terms become reversed in the Icelandic landscape. The prospect takes over to the extent that it redefines the spectator's stance as subject, and obliges us to locate subjectivity in the exploration and not the escape, if escape is indeed to be found. These places may demand a new basis for subjectivity, a remaking of the self. If, as Tuan suggests, our intimate and physical experience forms the basis for our spatial organization of the world and of our relation to it, what kind of self might these places reflect or create?

Grettir's persistent existence asserts a different concept of identity, forged and defined not solely by the "social" and at least partially by the "wild." It is not just that Grettir provides an ironic commentary on the failures of the social to civilize the forces of the "wild," whether these are found within or without society. In one of the most magnificent pieces of irony in the saga, at the site of the Hegranes *thing* or parliament at the bottom of Skagafjord (see figure 15), the disguised Grettir elicits an elaborate legal promise of a truce from the very group of farmers who are trying to remove him from Drangey; throwing off his disguise, Grettir holds them accountable to the law that will protect him, the outlaw. In this conundrum it is not only simple human rashness or stupidity, disordering forces from within, that negate the law, but the law is seen to negate itself. Grettir choreographs this process in order, once again, to survive.

I am not suggesting that Grettir somehow gives voice to the "wild"—to articulate it would be to delineate it within the bounds of the "social." Moreover, Grettir himself cannot control disordering forces from without, such as his own fear of the dark or the haunting gaze of the monster Glam. But I do think that the "wild," and specifically the wild as place, the places of the wild, gives shape, force, and motivation to his persona as a peculiarly Icelandic hero. He articulates the tension, for example, between ego-centered and society-centered perceptions of space that are fundamental to the Icelandic settlers' relation to their land and to the complex political and social development of that relation.

The extent to which it is possible to understand Grettir's relation to the wild in terms of an identity created by negotiation between self and place is an act and issue of definition that Grettir and the places he inhabits continually foil. He is the forest-goer who dwells in caves and valleys and islands, who traverses the spectral expanses of the lava fields and volcanic sands. He is the isolate male both seeking and rejecting connection, unable to come to terms with codes of social behavior and self-control and unable to bear being alone; he is continually trying to find a place to be, because, as he well understands, whether one is a superhuman hero or desperate outlaw, within or without social and legal worlds, one has to *be* somewhere. Grettir's stance and progress speak the dialectic between the center and the margin, and the instability and reversibility of both. To repeat: Grettir is finally a study in contradiction and uncontainability.

Gudrun Osvifsdottir

Grettir doesn't stay put, Gunnar will not leave, but Gudrun will not stay. Gudrun, the saga writer tells us, "was the loveliest woman in Iceland at the time, and also the most intelligent" (*Laxdæla Saga,* chapter 32). The saga chronicles her four marriages, none of which was to the man she ostensibly truly loved. Gudrun is unashamedly concerned with material possessions and social class; she is acutely conscious of status and of the bargaining in terms of money and land that attends the process of marriage settlement. Throughout the saga and the vicissitudes of her various marriages, she remains a respected, independent, and independently wealthy woman. Gudrun is exceptional, and recent critics, Jenny Jochens in particular, have taken up the question of whether she may be verging on the fantastic given the actual social and legal constraints on women at the time that the saga represents. Indeed, the whole question of the *degree* of reality, if any, that we may ascribe to this woman connects inevitably to the broader debate among saga scholars about the relation of the historical to the literary.[11]

Even within the saga we can see how Gudrun's relation to home and land might be complicated by a set of gender-related social variables. As the Icelandic man might define home in relation to the freedom to travel and a freedom of movement, the Icelandic woman's apparent exclusion from this mobility suggests a different relation. Gudrun, already married twice, has been courted frequently by Kjartan, to the extent that it was "common talk" in the neighborhood that they were a good match. Kjartan decides that he wants to travel and informs Gudrun, who is very displeased. Kjartan says that he will do anything to make her happy, but when she instantly replies that she wants to travel with him, he dismisses her request as simply "out of the question" (chapter 40), reminds her of her family responsibilities, and proposes instead that she wait for him for three years. Elsewhere in the sagas, women wait for their traveling betrothed or spouses to return. Their patience and stasis seem to be a cultural given; Gudrun's own son will later tell her that he wants to travel because he is "tired of sitting at home like a woman" (chapter 70). Gudrun, however, not only rejects Kjartan's proposal, but later marries Bolli, Kjartan's close friend and cousin, possibly out of a large dose of spite.

Two things stand out in my view throughout this part of the story. The first is that Gudrun's anger is rooted equally in her own incapacity to travel and overall lack of freedom of movement, and in her rejection by Kjartan; she is frustrated at the level of being denied personal freedom as well as receiving cavalier treatment from her lover. Her rejection is compounded if we accept Judith Jesch's suggestion that "Gudrun's request to Kjartan must be interpreted as a coded proposal of marriage, for that was the only circumstance in which she could possibly accompany him" (1991: 197).[12] The second is the "neighborly" quality of all of these interactions. Many of the homesites in this saga are within sight of each other (see plate 3, for example). Kjartan often visits Gudrun's home at Laugar, which is near the hot baths, and enjoys making these frequent visits for the pleasure of her conversation. There is much social backing and forthing, gossip and entertaining, criticism and backbiting, among this group of neighbors in Laxdale. Bolli finally kills Kjartan and is much later killed in turn, and Gudrun, who has taken no small part in inciting the various

Figure 16. View from Helgafell.

parties involved to vengeance, betrays no emotion. The extent to which this woman may be grieving for her husband becomes a matter for local debate and speculation. Gudrun's response is to move. Her friend Snorri offers to negotiate a settlement, but she does not want compensation for her husband's death. " 'I think, Snorri, that the best help you can give me,' she said, 'is to exchange homes with me, so that I don't have to live in the same district as the people in Hjardarholt' " (chapter 56).

Her social connections to home have eroded and finally destroyed any other connection to place. The land comes to represent social enclosure to her. Gudrun will find a new home and forge her connection to place independently of the socius, just as Gunnar does, notwithstanding the fact that Snorri's home at Helgafell, the "holy mountain," is far more bleak and remote (figure 16). Gudrun nicely confuses masculine and feminine patterns of relationship here; contrary to feminist critical assertions of a female psychology of self based on connection and constituted by interrelationship (see note 4 of this chapter), Gudrun is interested in severing the ties that bind, those of "home" and of social if not familial relationship (she does take the members of her immediate family with her). Gudrun is a woman of contradictions, and if the juxtaposition of a contemporary psychological viewpoint and a medieval Icelandic woman's decision making can tell us anything, it may be to encourage an examination of the ways in which the idea of Gudrun is born of contradiction on many levels.

Perhaps Gudrun is just heartily sick of her neighbors. Perhaps when she looks out on the stunning Laxriverdale landscape, she sees dust and ashes and failed love affairs. And perhaps, before I continue rewriting the saga, I should reexamine some of the assumptions of my scenario and uncover several further complicating elements in this intersection of places and selves.

I construct my story believing in Gudrun's autonomy and her freedom to change place, if not to move freely in the sense of travel. Elsewhere in the sagas, women *do* travel freely; consider Freydis, "the illegitimate daughter of Eirik Rauði, and a bad lot" (Marcus, 1980: 74), who sails off in Viking tradition to plunder and profit from the new world of Vinland (*Grænlendinga Saga,* chapter 8), or the more dignified Unn, who lays claim at the beginning of *Laxdæla Saga* to the entire territory within which Gudrun has the ostensible freedom to move, one woman creating boundaries for another.[13]

Ascertaining the degree of actual freedom for Icelandic women within and without the sagas is itself a dialectical problem, concerning micro and macro levels of social investigation. Carol J. Clover frames the questions and contradictions surrounding women's status in terms of the distinction between structural power, which belongs to the male, and dyadic power, which "has to do with the purchase one has in a one-on-one relationship" (1990: 125)—which in turn has to do with the sex ratio at any given historical point. Clover's thesis is that "settlement Iceland, thanks to its frontier status and female preferential infanticide, was short of women" (127), and this provides a demographic context in which we may expect to find some of the contradictions surrounding both female behavior and the way it is later narrated by the thirteenth-century saga writers (see note 11 of this chapter).

Clover describes a vicious circle where the success of the masculine Viking ideology of travel, warfare, and trade encourages parents to prefer sons to daughters, which promotes a higher rate of female infanticide, which then causes a sex ratio imbalance and the subsequent predictable set of variables and social ills characterizing communities with an excess of men: for example, institutionalized male violence, polygyny, male competition for women, male homosexuality, early betrothal of girls, high incidence of adultery, easy remarriage of women—all of which contribute to "a veritable roster of Icelandic saga themes and situations" (124).

Clover accounts for the apparent "uncontainability" (128) of women in the sagas by its opposite: the ugly fact of widespread female infanticide, which results in the increased dyadic social power of women. To what extent does this dyadic power affect structural power? To what extent do women control the domestic economy when Viking men are absent? Are these Icelandic women, left to organize the home front, forerunners of Rosie the Riveter? Clover argues that the expansion of women's informal or domestic/private powers correlates with a decrease in public, or structural, power, bringing us back to the core paradox: physical scarcity fosters political diminishment. The division of public and private spheres of power images the dialectic for us in terms of space and place, and it is interesting that recent research into gender domains reflects the same negotiation of micro and macro levels of spatial organization. Spatial domestic arrangements clearly reflect gender ideologies and male-female hierarchical arrangements; the spaces women occupy, those that they are "at home" in, those that they may claim legally or construct aesthetically, those whose production they control, these spaces are inscribed within and proscribed by kinship structures specific to social and economic structures (Gilchrist, 1988: 22). Recall the story in the first section of this chapter about the woman in labor "creating" her domain.

In context, however, spatial values are shifting: "Meaning does not adhere to the spatial frame, but must be evoked through action" (Moore, 1986: 186). One might recast the questions Clover addresses thus: Is the material base for patriarchal structuring of gender domains and activities changed or arranged sufficiently at the micro level to effect an imaginative or actual restructuring of gender domains at the macro level? Or, what constitutes Gudrun's particular historical and personal relation to space and place?

I wonder, for example, if Gudrun might have changed places with just anyone. Byock characterizes Snorri as a ruthless power broker and "master politician" (1988: 201); although he had settled his long-standing disputes in his home territory, he was leaving behind a complicated and embittered situation, as well as acting out of friendship for Gudrun—the reason he gives for agreeing to the exchange in the saga. But the apposition, or opposition, of Snorri's will to Gudrun's does not help us. Gudrun is not a player in Snorri's league. Snorri's "seat" has no political exchange value for a woman, even one such as Gudrun. Women did not exercise secular power in Iceland and were excluded from participation in the legal process, the cement of the social system (Byock, 1988: 134; Hastrup, 1985: 121). Despite his insistence that the central preoccupations of *Laxdæla Saga* are landownership and property deals, Byock's intricate analysis of Snorri's maneuverings elicits only a passing mention of

Figure 17. Gudrun's grave, with municipal railings.

Gudrun as part of the saga's "famous love triangle" (172). In fact, Snorri's historically verifiable and verified power as a *goði*, a "priest" or chieftain, highlights the fictional quality of Gudrun's power, although she too was a "real" Icelander. (I use "real" here in the sense that she has a grave, and is mentioned in chapter 84 of *Landnámabók* as a descendant of Bjorn the Easterner and Ketil Flatnose.)

The self that is Gudrun recedes, and so do the possibilities of understanding her connection to place, or rather, the layers of mediation make her increasingly opaque. Her existence as real or fictional character is further obscured by the historical record. I am reluctant, however, to see her "consigned to the realm of male fiction" where Jochens (1986: 50) would place these strong Icelandic heroines, or to fictionalize her further as a "literary cliché" (Jesch, 1991: 190). Gudrun's grave, marked (as few such sites are), stands out in curious, stubborn relief against the functional modern farm buildings and the municipal railings that now surround it (see figure 17 and plate 4). The journey we took from her first home at Laugar, over to Sælingsdale, and then on to the tiny iron-fenced chunk of hillside that is her grave at Helgafell, produced strong emotions and conjured a powerful presence, dignified and perhaps elicited by the onlooker's sense of place, of its power and presence. But I begin again to continue to write the saga, or rather to tell my own story.

Perhaps this is my only choice. My "search" for Gudrun serves to highlight the problem of reconstruction of women's lives when the available cultural record, both historical and literary, works to obscure rather than reveal; their remains might be just as profitably excavated, their trace identified, in the present realities of the places they inhabited in the past. When we opt for history as analogue, we are bound to tell a story, one that might fictionalize past selves and inevitably involve our present selves. It is no surprise, then, that I go looking for Gudrun and find my self in her stead, my self in place. But place, as I have said, is a relationship, a situating of the self; place is above all a negotiative activity, whereby we may extend, develop, or invent our dialogue with the past.

Places in Translation and the Metonymy of Terrain

We are all displaced, as any Freudian will tell us. Some are cast farther from the well-known place than others, however. Gunnar refused displacement, finding home worth more than life itself. Gudrun accepted it, finding home too problematic. Grettir accepted his legally imposed exile and turned his penchant for "ill luck," as King Olaf regretfully describes it in chapter 39 of *Grettir's Saga*, into valor, so that, as someone who had managed to inhabit a wilderness where habitation was thought impossible, he became associated forever with the *óbyggth*, the "undwelt-in" spaces of Iceland. Today, all across Iceland, even in places where Grettir never went in the saga, one finds huge boulders named for that strongest of outlaws, "Grettir stones," against which he is supposed to have tried his strength (see figure 18). A Grettir stone makes "the wilderness [rise] up to it, / And sprawl around, no longer wild," like the jar-crowned hill of Wallace Stevens's famous poem. At any rate, the human artifact or human name makes "the slovenly wilderness" (Stevens) seem less chaotic. The presence of the human and the known makes it accessible to our understanding, "translates" it. In this section I am going to discuss two things, as the title indicates: the effects of translation and of metonymy on our perception of place—or, to put it differently, how we tend to appropriate and appreciate an alien place, quite irrespective of its actual human history or lack thereof, by projecting our own desires and stories upon it. I shall begin autobiographically, illustrating the assimilation that takes place when two cultures touch.

I have been fascinated by cultural syncretism for as long as I can remember, but of course regarded it as "other," not as something that might be happening in my own life, my own poetry. In fact I started formally "translating place" a long time ago, about the time I first met

Figure 18. A "Grettir stone" near Grettir's home at Bjarg, upheld by the pastor from Midfjord.

Gillian. I was then a recently transplanted American determined to cast off past attachments and live in the England to which I was committed by marriage. I began translating poetry simply as a pastime, a form of consolation in an alien land. It was a way to immerse myself wholly in someone else's reality, giving my own a rest.

My husband, a British Wordsworth scholar, had been offered a post at a university in the north of England, on the threshold of Wordsworth's Lake District. What an opportunity! We left my tenure-track job in the United States, took my children out of school there, and went where the husband's job was without a hope of one for the wife. (It was a long time ago.) When we found Moulterbeck, the traditional seventeenth-century farmhouse that we had created in our imaginations, complete with stream flowing through the garden (the house once had a water mill), woods on the hill above, trout river below the home field, a big old cast-iron fireplace and bread oven that I recognized from Peter Rabbit books in the "living" room, the only warm room, truly it was not so bad . . . most of the time. It got better after we obtained space heaters and a dog, and after son David, deciding a farmhouse needed geese, ordered a half-dozen goslings in our name. That was a surprise, but not so surprising as the friendship that developed between me and the gander Gaiseric. (In the throes of studying sixth-form classics and irrespective of gender, David named all the geese after generals of antiquity. Spartan Brasidas turned out to be the best egg-layer.) Being there also became better after I started translating the Latin American poetry with which I was familiar. At first I translated just into English, then gradually into "Yorkshire," not the dialect but the terrain, wandering in the place with poems in my head.

I happened to know Spanish because when I was very little we lived in a Mexican mountain village; my Indian nanny knew no English. My younger brother is a true-born Southern Californian, and that is where we grew up, in foothills that were a paradise before the smog. Behind the house loomed Mount Wilson, where my father hiked, and in the valley below was the Huntington Library, where my mother researched. Most important for this essay was the place between, a big, sunny garden full of guavas, persimmons, and pomegranates, where my roots were. But when I had gone to live in Yorkshire forever, I had to draw up those roots and set them down in a beautiful, alien, cold land.

So I began translating—and varying and regendering—poems from a more familiar sort of terrain, and soon I was less displaced. From one of the poems from that time, from a book titled *Raíz Salvaje* (Savage root) by the Uruguayan Juana de Ibarbourou, a figure emerged to populate my barren landscape:

Song in the dark
pine boughs: a lark

Song of the bees aswarm
around the warm
gold of the honeycomb

Song of the miller's daughter
bathing long ago
in the river water . . .

81

She was a figure from the past who belonged in this landscape among the bees and pine trees where the poem itself had discovered her. She was similar yet additional to me. From the moment she emerged in this poem, the miller's daughter gave me company in that isolated farmhouse, along with my collie and the geese, during those long, dark days when husband and children were away.

Another poem turned the yellow seaside flowers of Neruda's famous ode into the stonecrop blooming gold against the slate roof of Moulterbeck, bringing home that faraway scene by something as simple as a flower name. Thus I learned to name some local wildflowers. (Few things make one feel more at home than calling the native flowers by name.) As I translated José Juan Tablada's "Yecan," his Mexican gods gave substance to the local mud-giant Yordas, said to haunt a nearby cave, and they revealed a Frozen Woman who screeches from limestone chasms. After I discovered her by indirection in Tablada's poem, this woman, too, began to "exist" for me somewhere around Black Shiver Moss up in Kingsdale, where the silvery arms of the single rowan tree are crushed by the stones that split and move in winter. Apart from revealing presences in the landscape, this activity of appropriating poetry to the terrain and vice versa actually enabled me to see more clearly my own physical surroundings. It also enabled me to embrace the reality before my eyes, as I projected alien poetry and personae, and my alien self, creating a pattern, weaving upon the landscape a place in which to belong. I legitimatized what I was doing with the term "translocation."

Translocation of this kind was precisely what that great twelfth-century writer Snorri Sturluson was doing when he invented—or else realigned—Iceland's four guardian spirits, beings supposedly native to that soil since the dawn of time. These four *landvættir* still guard those who live in their demesnes. They appear on the local banners, and to doubt their primeval indwelling is not only rude but threatening, for they mark out the psychic map that is Iceland. This is the tale that Snorri relates in the *Heimskringla* (1964: 173–74). King Harald of Denmark, thinking he might conquer the recently settled island, sent a warlock to spy it out. The warlock took on the shape of a whale and swam to Vapnafjord in the northeast corner of Iceland. A fierce dragon swooped out from the land and scared him off. "Away he backed from there," says Snorri, and as the warlock tries to land elsewhere, going north and west around the island, he encounters three other creatures, a "big bird," a bull, and a mountain giant, who guard the rest of Iceland. Finally he gives up and returns to Denmark, foiled.

The four creatures, bird, dragon, giant, and bull, quarter the land

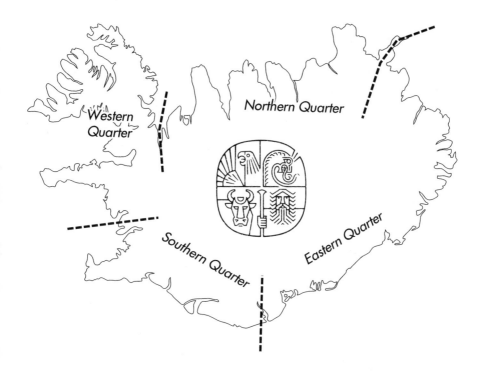

Figure 19. The *landvættir* and the quarters of Iceland, as portrayed by the logo of the Central Bank of Iceland.

among themselves. When one sees the *landvættir* on the handsomely designed Icelandic ten-kronar coin, or, as in figure 19, the logo of the Central Bank of Iceland, recognition leaps out. They recall the four winged evangelical beasts depicted on medieval crosses and gospel covers: the eagle of Saint John, the lion of Saint Mark, Saint Matthew's man, and Saint Luke's calf. (Iconographically, it was easy for the lion to become a dragon, because Byzantine art represented dragons as lion-headed.) This tetramorph, as the fourfold image is termed, was adopted to symbolize the four evangelists from Ezekiel's vision in the Old Testament (Ezekiel 1:4–10), and before Ezekiel similar figures were known in Assyrian art. Whether Ezekiel and Snorri were conscious of appropriating an ancient and authoritative image, or whether it appropriated them for its expression, is a moot point. By means of the ancient tetramorph Ezekiel established a tantric design for the meditation of future generations of Hebrews and Christians, and Snorri laid a grid of human meaning across his wild homeland.

Originary myths are useful for fixing identity and setting that fluid element, so vulnerable to contingencies, into a firmer symbolic dimension. When I discovered after her death a few years ago that what my well-brought-up mother had been doing in Mexico when I was a baby was running a gold mine, at a time when nice ladies didn't do that sort of thing, it gave me a tremendous sense of power over my own life, the feeling that I might also dare to go adventuring in ways that were not usual. Similarly, when Asser (1983: 67) traces King Alfred's genealogy back to the native god Woden and before him to Adam, by "recovering" such mythic origins he confirms Alfred's right to rule a kingdom of Germanic tribes that have been converted to Christianity (see also Sisam, 1953). Early Iceland presented a different challenge because it was ruled not by kings but by a representative council, thus having no royal dynasty for which mythic origins could be constructed. Another kind of myth was needed, one confirming that the land itself possessed an "ancient" and indwelling spiritual identity in which its new inhabitants could participate. As I mentioned in chapter 1, Egil Skallagrimsson in his saga points a rune-carved hex stake in the direction of his enemies the king and queen of Norway, enjoining the *landvættir* to drive them from their home—as they apparently do. Is this a proof that the concept of these indwelling spirits of the soil was native to Scandinavia, and part of the lore that the mainly Norwegian settlers brought with them to Iceland, or does it confirm our impression that Snorri wrote *Egil's Saga* as well as the *Heimskringla*? Whatever part of the myth Snorri invented, whatever he appropriated, it proved powerful, investing the land with significance to make it bearable, much as the miller's daughter bathing in the beck or the Frozen Woman in the Kingsdale crevice did for me. Even now, years and continents away, when I think of those figures from the Latin American poems I was translating, I "see" them against that Yorkshire landscape in which I placed them and to which I later became deeply attached. Myths make us feel at home, familiarized.

In his essay "Stalking with Stories," Keith H. Basso tells how certain Apache tales formulate a mutual relationship between land and story that invests the land with a *moral* significance, a meaning that requires wanderers to return home in order to find the world rightly shaped, or else to carry with them in their mind's eye the story place that is also home. They are "stalked by stories" about places they recognize so that, as one old woman puts it, "the land makes people live right" (1990: 100). This view of story as innately related to native place reminds us of Bruce Chatwin's theories about the Aboriginal "song lines" crisscrossing the outback of Australia, and extending, in his fantasy, across the whole inhabited world; and of Gary Snyder's "singing the mountains" (one runs one's voice along the contours of the mountain range, singing its ups and downs). Not all stories are so closely tied to the specific shapes of the land; some are more portable. Yet the original land contours inscribed in a story that is taken elsewhere may betray its origins, like the melody of one mountain range imposed upon another where it does not fit.

Such displacement may explain the difficulties encountered when imagining in situ the troll fights in *Grettir's Saga*, a displacement perhaps like singing the wrong mountain. In chapter 35 of the saga the problematic hero Grettir has slain and decapitated the possessed corpse of Glam, a revenant Swedish laborer who has been terrorizing a farm in Forsæludale. In another story in the saga, in chapters 65–66, Grettir, now legally declared an outlaw, takes on first a troll woman who has been haunting the farm Sandhaugar in Bardardale, and then another troll, presumably her mate, under the nearby waterfall. These two stories are Grettir's major encounters with supernatural beings, and it seems possible that the Glam story, woven integrally into the saga to provide the hero with a flaw (fear of the dark inspired by Glam's glaring eyes and his curse), has provoked the later troll story, which is not essential to the plot.

As has often been observed (most recently and clearly by Stitt, 1992), this later adventure with the two trolls is reminiscent of Beowulf's fights with humanoid monsters, first with Grendel and then with his mother, the first fight taking place in the Danish hall Heorot and the second in the monsters' hall under a lake. After Beowulf has torn off Grendel's arm, the cannibal monster staggers home to die, but his mother comes to Heorot for vengeance, renewing the feud, and Beowulf is obliged to fight again. Fred C. Robinson summarizes Beowulf's second battle as follows.

> He goes to the eerie tarn where the trolls lived together and dives to the bottom of it, as the ogress swims out and seizes him and drags him out of the water into her cave behind a waterfall. The two fight savagely, and Beowulf is about to be killed when he sees on the wall a giant sword, with which he kills the ogress and then decapitates Grendel, whose corpse is lying in the cave. (1991: 145)

Beowulf sees treasure, but comes back with only the giant sword hilt and Grendel's head, the latter to prove that the monster has really been slain. Beowulf nearly loses that fight below the waterfall because the weapon he brings with him, a sword called a *hæftmece*, fails, and when he emerges victorious the Danes who watched him dive into the tarn have left, thinking he has been killed.

Here is the similar account in chapter 65 of *Grettir's Saga*, quoted from the Fox and Pálsson translation:

> Then a great she-troll came into the hall. She carried a trough in one hand and a big cleaver in the other . . . They started grappling fierce-ly with each other, and fought for a long time in the hall . . . She dragged him out through the door . . . The ogress shoved him down to the river and all the way to the edge of the gorge. Although he was exceedingly weary, he had to fight even harder than before, or else let her throw him down into the gorge . . . At once he seized the short sword at his waist, drew it, and struck at her shoulder, slicing off her right arm. With that he was freed, and she dived down into the gorge and vanished under the waterfall. (1974: 137)

Grettir spends several days recovering from that fight, and then he goes back to the waterfall with the local priest.

> When they came to the waterfall they saw there was a cave down under the cliff. The cliff was so sheer that it could not be climbed, and it was almost ten fathoms [fifty to sixty feet] down to the water. They had brought a rope with them. (138)

Grettir says to the priest, "I am going to find out what there is in the waterfall, and you must look after the rope." But he is too sensible to trust his safety entirely to someone else, and secures the rope with a stake. Then he gets ready.

> He wore few clothes, and girded himself with a short sword, but had no other weapon. Then he plunged down from the cliff and into the waterfall. The priest glimpsed the soles of his feet, but had no idea what happened to him after that. Grettir dived under the waterfall. (139)

He comes up into a cave behind the waterfall, where a giant attacks him with a wooden-shafted pike. "Such a weapon was called a *hepti-sax*," says the saga (139). After a terrific fight, Grettir wins. He looks around and finds "a fair amount" of treasure and the bones of two men; he puts the bones into a bag, leaving the treasure, and swims back under the waterfall. He has to climb the rope by himself because the priest, think-ing him dead by now, has left.

Obviously the two stories have much in common—the plot, for exam-ple. In both stories there is first a fight in a house on land, in the course of which the hero takes off the arm of his foe, then a related fight where he has to dive underwater. Beowulf's opponents, however, are first male then female, whereas Grettir fights first the female troll and then the male. The detail that intrigues scholars most is the terminology for the weapons used in these two accounts. The Old English *hæftmece* and the Old Icelandic *hepti-sax* are each unique words in their own language and they seem semantically equivalent. The first elements *hæft* and *hepti* are cognate forms (Old English *f* answering to Old Icelandic *p*), and the second elements *mece* and *sax* are both terms for sword. The saga's "wooden-shafted pike" could be a sax or short sword affixed to a spearshaft for extended reach. Unfortunately, there is not enough evidence to come to any firm conclusions about these two related and unique words for weapons, so most commentators simply note their identity and posit a common source for both stories, Stitt preferring to relate both to the same mythic-heroic tradition. Yet more is to be observed here, an inversion along the same lines as the reversal of male-female opponents. In *Beowulf* the hero uses the *hæftmece*, which fails him, whereas in the saga the troll antagonist uses the *hepti-sax*. Grendel's mother possesses the only "sax" mentioned in *Beowulf* (at line 1545), as the troll does in *Grettir's Saga*. So what ways are these identities branching?

In the case of the landscape, differences and similarities between *Beowulf* and *Grettir's Saga* may equally be due to the way slippage and adaptation occur in a translated or translocated story, or discrepancies may simply be the result of the way we are reading. One gets the impression that the waterfall to which the troll wife drags and shoves Grettir is relatively near the farm Sandhaugar; others besides Gillian and myself have walked in that vicinity and have been disappointed to find only the little tributary Eyjardaleriver flowing tranquilly north of the farm, no ten-fathom gulf with a foaming waterfall. Yet major waterfalls are both upstream and downstream on the sizable river that flows down the length of the dale. Far away at the top of the dale the scenic waterfall Aldeyjarfoss plunges over basalt columns, and several kilometers down at the bottom of the dale is the picturesque Góðafoss, named for the images of pagan gods that the local priest threw into the falls (the *foss*) to mark his acceptance of Christianity a thousand years ago (see plate 5).

Majority opinion holds that the authors both of *Beowulf* and of *Grettir's Saga* probably heard similar story sequences in the oral tradition rather than that the saga writer knew about *Beowulf*. Wherever the *Grettir's Saga* author might have found his materials for the monster fights, they do seem to be imported to Iceland from the Scandinavian mainland and inserted in the saga as extra adventures. The hostile waterfall trolls especially seem designed to give Grettir something to do when wintering in Bardardale during his outlawry. But the waterfall in *Grettir's Saga* is located farther from the human habitation, and that in *Beowulf* nearer, than most of us imagine when engaged with these texts. In *Beowulf* we are told:

> The mountain river
> plunges down under the shadows of the headlands,
> a flood under the ground. It is *not far hence*
> in miles, that the lake stands.
>
> (1359–62; my emphasis)

And in *Grettir's Saga:*

> The ogress shoved him down to the river, and *all the way* to the edge of the gorge.
>
> (Chapter 65; my emphasis)

Both stories state clearly a distance in conflict with what we feel to be the case when reading.

Perhaps the pace of the storytelling itself accounts for the conflict. In *Beowulf* it takes twenty-two lines (1399–1421) to traverse the distance from hall to monster lake, and along the way the warriors meet the severed head of their friend; this encounter and the rhetorical description of their reaction considerably slow progress. In *Grettir's Saga* the trip takes just a few words, so progress over the landscape seems rapid. Whereas I feel that the *Grettir's Saga* author superimposes the landscape of the troll story directly upon the Bardardale terrain that he knows, with descriptions that deceptively give the impression of being less exact than they really are (though he does exaggerate Gódafoss into a fifty-foot plunge), Gillian believes that he had to manipulate the landscape considerably to accommodate the Beowulfian story. Once again the fit between story map and real map challenges our separate scrutinies. But beyond and irrespective of our map-reading, the real place, Bardardale with its flood-produced gravel mounds from which the farm Sandhaugar has taken its name for a millennium, is made more interesting and attractive for us by the story attached to it, or inlaid upon it, even though it is a story of hostile trolls. It seems as though the nature of the story does not matter so much as the fact that a place *has* a story. A place with a story is special, for those who live there and those who wander there alike.

"Such wandering is like an interrogation of the landscape," says Barry Lopez (in quite a different connection), as we try "by means of natural history and analog to pry loose from it a sense of a people who would be intimate with it" (1988: 173). "A sense of a people . . . intimate with it" is above all what we seek in this place. But we are doing more than inter-rogating the land. As Lopez says elsewhere, "The landscape seemed alive because of the stories" (1988: 63). Yet the Bardardale troll story is not integral to the place but imported, like Iceland's *landvættir* and those figures "discovered" in Yorkshire as the poems I brought there con-formed to the land I was living in. As the continental origins of its vivify-ing troll legend are revealed, by answering to and arguing with *Beowulf*, the Bardardale of *Grettir's Saga* itself becomes in a sense an author or a translator, certainly a mediator, participating actively in our discourse about places and translation.

These crossings and projections of stories upon the land betray a metonymic relationship between past and present, old land and new, and persons supposed to have been in the place where one stands now. Sometimes it is important simply to believe that you stand in "the very place."

Ardito Desio, the Himalayan expert and mountaineer, remarked in a television interview about the controversy concerning the comparative heights of Everest and K2 that "climbing the second peak in the world is different from climbing the highest peak in the world." This difference is entirely subjective. There is an emotional reward in attaining by great effort *what you believe to be* the uttermost point or "the very place." In "Sur," a story by Ursula Le Guin, an expedition of Chilean women reach-es the South Pole, another uttermost point but one not marked by any significant land formation and existing chiefly in the minds of mappers. Arriving there on December 22, 1909, the women put up their tent for only an hour's shelter in which to have a cup of tea, then they strike camp and set out north again, homeward. After incredible hardships they arrive back safely, and never tell anyone of their feat. When Amundsen's expedition reaches the South Pole in 1912, the narrator enjoins her grand-children, for whom she is now writing down her experience, that "they must not let Mr. Amundsen know! He would be terribly embarrassed and disappointed" (Le Guin, 1983: 271). This story is a feminist's exploration of ways that the female interest in travel and terrain may be different from that of the male; the fame attached to attaining the distant and difficult is not paramount for these women. In fact, even being there is a disappointment to them, as in one sense it must be to anyone: there is nothing to see at the South Pole. But most explorers would nevertheless find a satisfaction in achieving the ultimate "point" for its own sake. My brother and I have entertained the idea of walking the Arctic Circle; we even looked up the distance on the globe, just because it seemed like "a neat thing to do" (his words). It turned out to be far too long to be feasible, so then we turned to the Antarctic Circle. Because most of that imaginary circle crosses ocean, the walking would not be so far. Is that a good way to spend the rest of our life's summers (or in the Antarctic, winters)? Why even consider it? Why are those imaginary circles upon the landscape of interest? Why, to return to the subject of this book, should one wish to try to work out, and then visit, the location of imaginary Beowulf's homeland, or the Bardardale of a scarcely more real outlaw?

I remember a story, perhaps an Arthurian romance: A maiden goes to sleep and has a dream in which she is visited by a prince who gives her a ring. He tells her that when she is in trouble she must turn the ring on her finger and he will help her. She wakes up and finds that she is wearing the ring. Stories like this are told with many variations, and they are almost always effective, just as the opposite—a vivid adventure concluded by the protagonist's waking up to find it was *only* a dream (as in the movie *The Wizard of Oz*)—can kill the story. I propose that the one works and the other does not because of the way we read or listen to stories. Peter J. Rabinowitz suggests that as we read a work of fiction we occupy two simultaneous roles in relation to the story, as *authorial* audience and as *narrative* audience. He explains that we as authorial audience know, along with the author, that the work is a fiction, whereas we as narrative audience believe, along with the narrator inside the story, in the truth of the story. "As a result," he says,

> the aesthetic experience exists on two levels at once. We can treat the work neither solely as what it is nor solely as what it appears to be; we must be simultaneously aware of both aspects. We are hardly responding adequately to *Romeo and Juliet* if we leap on stage to warn Romeo that his beloved is not really dead. Neither, however, should we refuse to mourn Juliet because we know that once the curtain falls she will be up and partying with the rest of the cast. The proper response treats *Romeo and Juliet* as both "real" and "unreal" (or both "true" and "untrue") at once. (1981: 410)

This helps to explain why the protagonist's discovery on waking up that the dream ring is real, when the authorial audience has known she was dreaming, has such a positive impact on the narrative, whereas the protagonist's merely waking up from a dream, the authorial audience having assumed that the narrative was to be understood as real, is so disappointing. The first case, of the dream ring's being real, serves as a metaphor for the fiction itself; if the maiden woke up to find the ring so surprisingly on her finger, perhaps there is hope that we, the authorial audience so firmly excluded from entering the world of fiction, may likewise have a chance to touch that world in some way. The journey to Oz that turns out to be a dream (only in the movie version) both insults our intelligence at the level of the authorial audience—we already knew it was not real—and undermines the engagement of the narrative audience that was actually there with Dorothy.

When dealing with the literature of another time or culture, however, an additional complication of the audience role must be considered. There is, if one may extend Rabinowitz's metaphor, a triple audience: the authorial audience aware of reading a text, the narrative audience participating in the fiction, and the culturally removed audience that is aware of its own alterity. For the medieval storyteller's ideal audience, for example, alterity would not be an issue and the story would be "natural" in ways it cannot be to us. We might call that ideal audience the *original audience* (as opposed to us, the *alien audience*), siting it in the storyteller's own world.

Here is an example that may be useful. To someone like myself, reading far away from Europe about an Arthurian romance or even reading a modern retelling of an Arthurian tale, it makes very little difference whether the story takes place in Wales or Broceliade or Narnia. The alien audience is already of the opinion that this is fantasy, dreamtime, the landscape invented, and the same audience as narrative audience relates to the story and accepts it on those terms. The authorial audience aware of reading is distanced (we Americans know that Arthurian Wales is a fantasy land), the narrative audience accepts; as good readers we can embrace the dichotomy and accept the alterity, just as we can accept man-eating trolls as part of a medieval story. But to someone reading or listening in the actual location where the story is set, as the original audience of medieval literature often was, description of place has an entirely different impact. Then the response of the authorial audience becomes closer to that of the narrative audience. By means of *the metonymic contiguity of place,* the audience outside the story that looks on benevolently but withholds belief begins to merge with the audience that has a spectral existence inside the story along with the narrator, for whom the characters, events, and physical world of the story are real. The story world's alterity is thus subverted by the simple means of familiarity with its landscape.

In going to the location where a story takes place and being receptive there once again to the story's projections, one engages a double or triple audience in the self. It is possible to make objective scholarly discoveries about the story and its terrain, but such scholarly, disinterested discoveries have little to do with what our going to Iceland and reading the sagas there was really about for me and Gillian, or what sailing in the wake of Beowulf was about on our Cattegat voyage, or what the point of the journey will be for most of those who may use our plotting out of these locations to go there themselves.[14] Such effort has much more to do with our roles as narrative audience, seeking to relate to, not analyze, the story. It places both us and the characters of fiction within the same physical space. Of course it does this differently from the way entering the story world occurs when we engage with a text imaginatively while reading it. As the engaged narrative audience of a text, we are spectral watchers in a reality more vivid than we are, whereas when we reread the text at the place of the story, going "native" in the sense of putting ourselves in the position of an imagined original audience, we are concretely as present as the place is, while the story people enter the scene spectrally, like well-remembered friends who have truly existed there and are now absent. The link is the place, revivifying the story and renewing our pleasure in the text.

Just now Gillian read to me a passage that she is putting into her account in the final chapter, about pulling herself up the final length of chain to get onto the top of the island Drangey (see plates 9 and 11). I relaxed and listened, engaging with her story. As narrative audience I was there with her, my vision of the place enhanced by my having been on the real island, and the vicarious experience was lovely, even though in her story she was scared to death. Then she mentioned Grettir, and his going up the frayed rope that was hanging there in his day, and I saw him, too. Grettir and Gillian had an equal density against the remembered rock face. They seemed equally real to my awakened imagination.

I know *Beowulf* is a story. Although at the center of that story is the fantasy of trolls and dragons that Tolkien so loved and his predecessors disparaged, plenty of the details of history and material culture in the poem have been shown to be probable. I believe that the locations are, if not provable, equally probable, and I and others have argued the case with the usual scholarly reticence in learned journals. Those attempts to prove the feasibility of selecting one site over another certainly bear on the intensity of feeling evoked by the places themselves; if we did not believe it legitimate to project the story folk onto these particular landscapes, the places would have little meaning for us, even less than Ardito Desio's second-highest peak. Most of us have known the disappointment of going to a site and then finding that it was not where the battle took place (or that it was not the highest peak in the world or the Simplon Pass). The disengaged and objective authorial audience must be pacified in order for the narrative audience to have a chance at engagement. But once the gates of possibility are opened, the flood of belief may be allowed to enter. Like waking up with the ring on your finger, it is joyful to stand where you can imagine Gudrun "really" standing on a sunny day, watching for her lover Kjartan to come riding that well-known road to Laugar, or to wait with Wealhtheow and Hrothgar for their Danes and those visiting Geats to return from Grendel's mere. It is joyful, a little more mutedly perhaps, to stand on that headland of Weder Isle Fjord where maybe twelve riders once circled a cairn, lamenting their lord. In such places, the text that was fiction takes on a different form. It becomes not a remembered text, but memory itself, a memory of some-thing that *was* as we stand in the place of the story, joined with those others who lived and loved and fought and died there, by the metonymy of our mutual terrain.

CHAPTER 3

The Saga of the Saga

We had originally planned to cowrite a conclusion in which we would narrate our own "saga." We had imagined an anecdotal travelogue, set in the context of the epic and saga landscapes that we had traversed, and informed by contemporary thinking about women, autobiography, and place. Our "saga" was to be a self-conscious examination of our own life journeys seen in relation to the northern medieval "landscapes of our desires." As usual our practice has revised our theoretical intention, and we plan now to attempt both more and less—and other—than we had intended. As our second journey in Iceland progressed, it developed a kind of independent momentum, a life of its own in which we began to see ourselves as observers and participants. The journey became characterized, organized, even controlled by the idea of Grettir, his life and his death, and the places in which these were enacted. The intensity of our "search" for Grettir may have been a result of the fact that we narrowly escaped with our own lives early in the trip. It may have been occasioned by any number of factors, the intersecting presence and power of places and histories, both literary and personal, but this particular intensity brings us to focus our concluding "saga" on Grettir, and the coming together of so many different kinds of information and emotion that leads us to retrace here the road to Drangey (see figure 20). We traveled this road together but we arrive at and define our destinations differently, and so we present two accounts of the paths that each of us discovered to the island where the hero dies.

The Road to Drangey

On our first joint journey to Iceland we did not have time to go to Drangey; it wasn't in the plan, not on the program. Staying on the main ring road, we drove within fifteen or so kilometers of Skagafjord, and Marijane, with an unusual degree of longing and melancholy, called attention to a distant speck in the water. She was disappointed to pass this

Figure 20. The road to Drangey.

way yet again and not make the trip to the island. I thought no more of it; Grettir's peculiar attractions had not yet taken hold. When planning our second trip together, it became increasingly obvious that Marijane believed that getting to Drangey was to be the focal point, the "mission" of our research and reinvention, but at this point the journey to Drangey still made only logical and academic sense to me. It was the documented place where the hero had survived for a time and then met his death.

I had read the saga and knew that Drangey was remote and difficult of access, and that Grettir and his companions "liked it on the island" (chapter 74). From the *Iceland Road Guide,* a cryptic text in many respects, I had learned that it was a rocky island "grassy on top, difficult to climb" (1981: 273). These "facts" began to take on a degree of reality in a coffee shop in the center of Reykjavik. A friend of Marijane, an educator, an intellectual, an influential political activist, a woman to admire, a woman not young but full of energy, produced a stack of photographs and talked animatedly about the journey to Drangey she had made a few weeks before. She said the trip was the hardest thing she had done in her life, physically and mentally. Her face flushed with satisfaction and triumph as she recounted not believing she could make it and finding out that she could. I looked at the pictures, the rough seas, the sheer rock faces, the dizzying heights, the tense anorak-clad figures in various poses, buffeted by the wind or huddled at the summit, and felt a burst of pure terror.

In later conversations, when I confessed this response, she would tell me that such fear was quite warranted, that many of the local people would never consider going to the island. They watched tourists blithely attempt the climb and themselves stayed put, aware of the dangers and the history of past deaths and accidents, when local "egg-takers," groping for seabird eggs on the cliff faces, had misjudged the sheer rock walls. At the time I tried to show an intellectual interest in the coffee-shop discussion and not betray my apprehension. But I was thinking of my light-weight walking shoes packed in place of boots, and I thought of how I had underestimated Iceland again and possibly overestimated my own powers of physical endurance, how I should have known better. Coming more clearly into focus, more as a question than a resolution, was also the notion that Grettir *liked it there*; this place suited him.

Apparently, it also suited Marijane, who began to hatch a plan to sleep overnight alone on the island. Fortunately, and conveniently, we have different areas in which we are each either hesitant or unafraid. I will ride a horse almost anywhere and enjoy driving along the steepest road that edges a glacial river. Marijane prefers to do neither, but is undaunted at the prospect of scaling the side of an island of rock that rises perpendicularly from the crashing waters beneath. My own ambivalence about going to this place began here; perhaps I began to displace my own fear onto the idea of Grettir, and developed a wariness and ambivalence about the hero and my relation to him. Going to Drangey became one of those things that you have to prove to yourself that you can do, satisfying and unpleasant in equal proportions, and I did not then question the automatic way in which I took up this challenge, nor did I question the externally validating motivations for it. I knew that I was uncomfortable with the whole idea, that I was resisting being controlled by and was in some vague and petulant sense blaming Grettir, a series of fictions—the hero included—that seemed ridiculous enough to dismiss. Marijane, however, grew progressively more enthusiastic about the trip and the hero, and more committed to the idea of sleeping alone on the island—in order, she explained unconvincingly, to dream Grettir's dreams.

On the first day of our "search" for Grettir, we drove north from Reykjavik; we had been looking for Grettir's hideout in Fagraskogafell (see plate 2) but light drizzle had prevented us from seeing or photographing much. We were about to give up and return to the main road when we overturned our rented car on a sharp curve. After a balletic slow-motion somersault, our car bounced carefully back to stasis and we discovered that we were basically unharmed, though definitely upside down. In the minutes passing as we tried to disengage ourselves from the car, one

Icelander had already phoned for help. The usual period of police, questions, and insurance followed, and within four hours we were on the road again in a new car, an exact replica of the old one, with an injunction from the rental-car agency to bring this one back in one piece.

The story of our accident is ordinary and bizarre, dramatic and matter of fact, a combination that we did not know how to place as we sat, clearly in a state of mild shock, in the service-station restaurant, waiting for the new car to be delivered. Should this "brush with death" be included in our saga? And what did it have to do with Grettir? At the least we continued our journey with a much-heightened sense of the danger that Iceland presents, and we were glad to be alive. Several days later, embroiled in what became an involved and drawn-out process of trying to get to Drangey, we further hypothesized our relation to fate, to death, and to Grettir. I had begun to feel that the gods were either crazy or at play. "I think Grettir did it," decided Marijane, "because it terrified us but didn't hurt us. Typically Grettir." Just like his treatment of Gisli, whom Grettir chases and terrifies, and who runs furiously even as he is stripping down to his underclothes. Did we, unlike Gisli, retain any dignity, I wondered? The site of our accident was familiar to police and passers-by; cars flipped over at the spot with some degree of regularity— "at least once a week," one kindly policeman said. The gallant Icelander who phoned from his car for help had overturned a jeep at the very same place. Had it not been for the oddly abstracted reality of death escaped, defied, the whole incident might have smacked of burlesque. Later we found out that we had made second-page news in the Reykjavik newspaper; a picture of the overturned car was accompanied by copy that marveled over the luck of two unnamed motorists.

Luck and survival, overlaid with a fluctuating sense of controlled and controlling irony. These key elements of Grettir's story figured prominently in ours. Getting to Drangey, a journey I was already dreading, became a kind of dance, one step forward, two steps back . . .

In Reykjavik we had tried to arrange a boat to take us to Drangey but had been told by numerous agencies that this would be best organized when we arrived at Skagafjord, and that we should talk to the "Drangey man," Jon Eiriksson. We phoned from Reykjavik and Marijane informed Eiriksson, who seemed skeptical but amiable, of her intention to camp out on the island. My strong impression was that he did not take the plan, or us, seriously. By coincidence, if one believes in such things, Eiriksson ran a guesthouse at his farm at Fagranes, on the edge of the fjord south of Reykir and directly within sight of Drangey. We changed our previous plans and arranged to stay there for two, three, four days. We weren't sure, we told him; it would depend on how long it took to get to Drangey.

When we arrived in the Skagafjord area we initially tried to expand our options and shopped around for Drangey expeditions. This was no casual tourist boat trip, apparently. Three or four separate inquiries of hotel managers, fishermen, and locals in the fjord all pointed us in the direction of the "Drangey man," but the problem then became *sighting* the said Jon Eiriksson. We arrived at Fagranes at dusk, our first sight of the island dramatized by a respectable sunset, certainly forbidding though by no means as spectacular as the black-rock-set-against-blood-red-sunset postcards that I sent the next day. "I am about to sail here," I wrote, as I looked at the postcard image and then out at the real thing the next morning. The real thing loomed as a blur on the horizon, hardly visible through squalls of wind and rain. We were not going to Drangey that day.

Laying eyes on the "Drangey man," then persuading him to take us to the island, and waiting for the right weather, became the primary occupations of the next several days. Naturally, all these delays fed my apprehension directly. On the third day, we met Jon Eiriksson, returned from his multiple fishing and farming pursuits. (I later understood his constant activity to be a normal part of many Icelanders' summers; the "season," both tourist and agricultural, is short, and Icelanders' annual income in many instances depends on making the most of these few months.) He greeted us at the door of his farmhouse, shook our hands, looked us both squarely in the eyes, and said, "You will go to Drangey?" His intonation resulted in a perfect balance of question and statement, of mild mockery and faint disbelief. To have to struggle through these layers of ambiguity, I thought, to get something I'm really not sure that I want. I smiled faintly in response. Marijane enthusiastically assented.

But before we could discuss the time of the trip, its cost, the weather forecast, all the things that I would have been more comfortable being able to nail down, interested as I was becoming in the smallest pieces of certainty, we were told to sit down. First we had to watch the video. At ten in the morning, in a remote Icelandic farmhouse, the sun finally appearing (why couldn't we just go now, I thought), we sat in a darkened room and watched a replay of the experience we might be about to have. Most memorable and bizarre was the zither—or possibly balalaika—accompaniment; the boat to Drangey bobbed merrily on the waves to music reminiscent of the Greek islands and *Doctor Zhivago*. We watched the boat arrive, we watched the cheerful passengers climb, first, almost vertical shale paths, then the absolutely vertical rock face (with the help of chains to parallel Grettir's use of a ladder); we saw them triumphantly arrive at the top. We saw further dramatic shots of Jon Eiriksson, one of the foremost egg-gatherers in the region, rappelling freely and skillfully along the sheer cliffs and collecting eggs from the puffins' nests. Occasionally the camera would veer down, to remind the audience of the distance between summit and sea. I had by this time decided that the only way I would make it would be with my eyes closed.

Having seen the video we were dismissed, apparently for the day, and no further indication was made of when or whether we would go to Drangey. As Jon Eiriksson spoke little English, and Marijane was doing most of the communicating, I was obliged to accept the pace of negotiation, which seemed to me to be what was happening. Marijane and I rationalized and responded to the situation quite differently. Later that day I observed her in deep conversation with the farmer, who was poring over his tractor engine. Good, I thought, now we will find out when and how much and how long. But the conversation had been about the difficulties of fixing tractors and reminiscences on Marijane's part about how her father used to love to fix things. Eiriksson reminded her of her father, she said, and of yet another father of a friend of hers with whom she had once toured northeast Iceland. The importance of anyone's father in our present situation had not yet occurred to me, and I told Marijane so. We disagreed as to the best method of how to achieve our objective—getting to Drangey. I suggested the direct and unsubtle approach, when and how much money, we have deadlines to meet, and so forth. She preferred what seemed to me a less direct method of negotiation, of encouraging an almost paternal responsibility in Eiriksson, who was both our captain and our host. I felt that this was manipulative even as we were being manipulated, although in retrospect I see how we were both already individually negotiating with some idea of the father, how Drangey, Grettir, Sylvia Plath's Daddy, and Freud's Father and his Lacanian incarnation were all becoming increasingly less theoretical.

Marijane's way was wholly successful. The following afternoon the weather cleared and we set out for the island. Not only did she persuade Jon Eiriksson to leave her overnight on the island, which he had been loath to do given the uncertainty of the weather (she could be there for a week, he had warned), but he also, to my jaw-dropping amazement, carried her weighty pack, water supply and all, up the truly vertical slopes of Drangey. I could not complain too much about this victory of the Father, or criticize Daddy and daughter for playing out their respective roles, because of my own intense relief that I didn't have to carry my camera with its heavy wide-angle lens; Marijane, chivalrous in her turn, offered to do so and I gratefully accepted.

Of course the reality was not as bad as my worst imaginings, but the ascent was nonetheless scary, and in places my heart pounded so loud and fast that I was oblivious to everything else. I took no photos of the ascent; I could not spare the energy or the concentration. On the last part of the climb, I felt truly heroic, clinging to a chain suspended from the summit and scrambling up the sheer rock face in zigzagging, highly unstable fashion. Then came a blessedly stationary iron ladder, by means of which the traveler scales the last dozen or so feet of the ascent, and scrambles up onto the wildly lush grass of the island's surface. Grettir, of course, used no iron ladders or chains, but a simple rope ladder. Once standing shakily and victoriously on the top, I did succeed in taking a picture of that reassuring ladder (see plate 11). Let me contextualize my heroism by adding that we were accompanied on the climb by a family of Icelanders; three young teenagers and their mother had enough largesse and energy remaining from their own efforts to ask me at several junctures if I was doing all right. I noted that these were, at least, Icelandic children, and not garden-variety foreign tourists.

If Marijane had been right, then so was Grettir. The island, once scaled, is remarkably pleasant. It is a small, humanly manageable area; strangest of all, it feels safe. Looking over to the mainland, Grettir's four-mile swim to Reykir to bring back fire comes into perspective, into the realm of imaginable possibility, though being able to imagine that he could have made it does not seem to detract from the grandeur of its heroic impossibility. The remains of Grettir's dwelling curve and nestle into a fold of one of the valleys of deep lush grass, fertilized by centuries of generations of birds. He lived well on seafowl and eggs, the saga says. Isolated but protected, a superb vantage point though vulnerable in its isolation, its good points are also its bad points—rather like Grettir, I mused. I am standing on the perfect metaphor, I thought, recalling how much has been written about the psychological aptitude of this location. But Grettir lived here, found a living here for four years, and Grettir died here, of poison, magic, and treachery, so the saga goes. I replaced the metaphor with my own experience of the fictions of the saga and the realities of place. There was nothing metaphorical about the power of this place, invested as it had become with my own fear and relief, and my unexpected but intense pleasure in its beauty.

We left Marijane happily alone on the island, and sailed back through one of those blood-red postcard sunsets. The descent had been just as difficult as the ascent, but my perspectives on both danger and Grettir seemed to be rearranging themselves. Although the following day began with strong winds and rain, it cleared up enough for Jon to make the trip

Figure 21. View of Drangey from the hot springs at Reykir.

back later that afternoon, retrieving a rather indignant Marijane, who was growing accustomed to the island's particular brand of solitude. She said she slept soundly and dreamed not at all. I had spent the day riding down to the hot springs at Reykir (see figure 21) where Grettir ostensibly bathed after his swim, and where he was insulted by the serving woman who in turn bore a greater insult from him, a rape casual in its enactment and its narration (see note 3 of chapter 2). Remembering this easy violence, setting it next to his impressive capacity as a swimmer, and looking back out to the island from astride a sturdy Icelandic horse, my own more secure vantage point, my ambivalence toward Grettir reasserted itself.

When Marijane returned that evening, we began a discussion of events that was to continue throughout the remainder of the trip and into these two accounts of "the road to Drangey." We had made it to Drangey, and back, but to add "safely" would be to invoke our own accident, our "luck," and the vagaries of fate in the form of Jon the "Drangey man" and the weather. The direction and conclusion of our journey had been, in many places, out of our hands, and this fluctuating relation to controlling or being controlled prompted an analysis of its ambiguity. I thought that the "Drangey man" knew exactly what he was doing, and that he had been playing with us. Marijane discounted any manipulative intent but conceded that he was at play, as many Icelanders are, with the range of possibilities that the day will bring. "Come when you like and we'll see how it is," I had been told by his daughter when trying to make arrangements to rent a horse to ride to Reykir. When I paid my bill, I discovered that the horse rental was substantially less than I had expected. "Er, is this all right?" I queried, suspecting that it might be a mistake. "Is it all right with *you*?" said the Drangey man with the same intonation that he had met us with that first morning, a perfect balance between question and statement.

And what had this relation to ambiguity to do with the object of our exercise, the hero Grettir, the figure who had led us this dance? Marijane and I were both ambivalent about him and tried to understand why. "Is it that nasty horse business?" she asks, alluding to the young Grettir's savage treatment of his father's prize mare. Marijane trivializes while epitomizing the gratuitous violence, and its easy dismissal or casual glorification, that is so troubling to me. No, I reply, in an intentionally different register, it's death-centered masculine desire. I had recently completed a theoretical reading of *Beowulf* that involved a feminist critique of heroism, and such phrases sprang easily to mind. Theoretically pretentious—or perhaps merely inappropriate—as this sounded while eating canned soup and viewing Drangey from the security and comfort of our guesthouse, the issue insistently recurs.

I was once asked by a genuinely puzzled colleague, who knew of my theoretical and feminist interests, why I did what I did, that is, study heroism so intently and travel around in the wake of so many male heroes. What's the fascination? she wanted to know. A parallel question was raised when I first presented a paper on the "unmannerly" Queen Modthryth in *Beowulf,* and the respondents argued that any feminist approach must *of necessity* be hostile to Beowulf, to the masculine heroic ideal, and to the masculine world of the poem overall. I was shocked. Hostile to Beowulf? Me? Who was so fascinated by and drawn to his world, and as a consequence so motivated to understand the terms of that fascination? I might add here that one reviewer has since suggested that my statements of how exciting the poem can be "border on the genuinely hysterical" (Tripp, 1990: 77), although the same critic claims to detect a "hatred of the heroic" (76) in my work and that of others who question or deconstruct heroic values. My response has been to try to attenuate and dismantle the binary thinking that dictates one or the other, one at the expense of the other, and to examine how to coexist critically, and as a feminist critic, with the ambiguities of the masculine heroic world. Part of the attraction of Beowulf for me is that he is a thinker, capable of sociability and tact, and that he suffers, if not from modern neuroses, then certainly from recognizable forms of introspection and self-reflection. The hero is one of the most unsettling forces in the poem, generating ambiguity toward the masculine heroic ideal even as he functions as its epitome.

But what about Grettir? Njal makes sense, declares Marijane, he is admirable now for the same reasons he was then, a law-giver, a voice for social order and reconciliation. But how can we, as women, justify admiring Grettir? We try to pinpoint what it is that is so compelling about him, and even as I am turning over in my mind the ghoulish and compromising aspects of being drawn toward an exclusively masculine ideal that I perceive as death-driven (at least in the sense of heroism's overwhelming demand for decisive action, closure, and resolution), I conclude once again, along with Marijane, that what is so attractive about Grettir is that he stays alive. His strength certainly meets standard heroic specifications, and he is perhaps no more or less repugnant than that other "heroic" Icelander Egil Skallagrimsson, but his capacity to survive is finally his most memorable and impressive attribute. True, he meets his death on Drangey, but I recalled some of those places—those we had succeeded in gaining access to—where he roamed as an outlaw for about fifteen years. Their power to subdue the body and the imagination evokes the presence of the hero, and demands our respect for Grettir's powers of survival.

The question remains of whether the shadow of masculine desire—the power of Grettir to draw me in, or the power of the "Drangey man" to transform us into instant daughters—eclipses or denies our present and individual desire, or whether these places in which I enact and conjure past desire are grounds of mediation, as I try to define my present desire in, for, and through the landscape. Place becomes as much the terrain for negotiation between masculine and feminine as it is for other culturally and historically designated oppositions. Drangey brought me face to face with the ambivalence, fear, and fascination of my own desire, as this was structured and informed by the past, by history and fiction, and as it is produced in the present in so many ways, not the least of which is the experience of place. Drangey required, encouraged, the possibilities for negotiation between them.

The experience of Drangey suggested above all that there must be—and that there is—plenty of room for ambiguity, and that Grettir's past places were those of present possibility. We left Skagafjord and headed toward Grettir's birthplace at Bjarg; the overriding imperative of getting to Drangey, and not chronology and synchrony, had directed our itinerary. The weather was poised to surprise us: one half of the sky was brilliantly clear, the other gray and foreboding, with a place across the center—almost a line—where the two met (see plate 6). I remarked that we had a perfect fifty-fifty chance of absolutely anything. I meant the weather, but Marijane expanded the frame of reference by recalling our overturned car and the sunset on Drangey, and I agreed.

Where's Grettir?

One of the nicest things about God is that He is not exactly present. Even if we accept the idea that He is immanent, we really think of Him, most of us, as being up there beyond the stars, saying, "Let there be light," and there is light. The Goddess, on the other hand, is right down here in the midst, stirring us up, saying, "Let there be desire!"

And there is desire, burning and overwhelmingly present. My road to Drangey was different from Gillian's mainly in that respect: she had an intellectual agenda, whereas I had *lust*. She wanted to check out, I wanted to be in, the places where a thousand years ago Grettir the Strong had been. We were following up our idea that in the Icelandic sagas, more than in most other European fictions, the presence of the landscape makes a difference in how the story is imagined, because the people in these particular "frontier" fictions are interacting with the terrain as well as with each other. Certainly that is the case with Grettir, whose greatest claim to fame is that he survived for so long as an outlaw, that is, in the wild and desperate outbacks of Iceland, apart from society. Wild and desperate, yes, but in the summertime when we were following in Grettir's footsteps, the Iceland we encountered even in the lava- and glacier-wrought violence of the *óbyggth*, the uninhabited lands, was exquisite with grassy hollows of incredible greenness—brief green against aeons of bleak stone, softness against the long rock. Winter does not bear thinking about.

We were looking at Grettir's "attuned space," as the German philosopher Elisabeth Ströker might call it. Attuned space "has an appropriate mode of coexistence with the lived ego," and thus "escapes all the conceptual determinations of a thought founded on the opposition of object and subject" (Ströker, 1987: 19). It seems to me that Ströker has something here (as I read her) that I can use. Just as we all partake of the spaces in which we function, Grettir *is* his space. His space is Grettir. Yet, imagining him gone, I feel perfectly comfortable about appropriating his summertime space as my own. Though I have entered it with academic backing on the understanding that I am "doing Grettir," I feel no qualms about being here on my own behalf, once I am here, even though my lust for this space is the opposite of Grettir's. As an outlaw, he must find "home" (attuned space) in the wilderness. As my somewhat anarchic but nevertheless law-abiding and law-protected self, I am attracted to Grettir's space by the very fact that it is alien, jangling. I am attracted specifically to Drangey, that lava island on the edge of the world, because it is "afloat" in the margin between so many things, the here and the there, the known and the alien, the living and the dead. The spoken and the unspoken. My fear is that in writing this essay I might ruin the power of the unattuned space that is Drangey.

Drangey: Drang Isle, the translators call it. The Icelandic word *drangi* means, according to my dictionary, "(detached) pillar of rock," and that indeed is the nature of Drangey, a rock at the edge of the world, detached. Puffins, those strange fat birds, lay their eggs in the crevices of sheer cliff, and in the springtime egg-gatherers rappel down from the cliff tops as they have done for centuries. Actually, the island is named for the Kerling, the "old woman" of rock who stands separate from the main island, jutting up into the icy waters like a black old hag, formidable, a minion of the Goddess saying, "Stay off!" (See plate 7.) But she has the opposite effect on my desire: I *must* get onto that island. Moreover, I must be alone there fully to be there, for Drangey is potentially the most alien space I can get to, and the presence of companions would destroy its otherness. Even as I write this I remember in my very genitals that intense wish to be alone on Drangey, a flood of desire that in former days was associated only with a need to be in the beloved's arms, never with this strangely sexual lust for, of all things, solitude in an uninhabited space.

When did the question of getting to Drangey first come up? I guess it was initially voiced during the first trip that Gillian and I made to Iceland together, when we decided reluctantly, in our whirlwind tour of the sagasteads of Iceland, that we could not possibly get to Drangey in the limited time we had. We achieved only a fleeting glimpse of the island as we sped from Grettir's birthplace in Middale to the haunted farm in that Dale of Shadows off Vatnsdale, where he fought troll-like Glam. On that trip we were locating only the spaces of Grettir's major actions; we had no time for his place of death. On the second trip, however, death demanded our attention right at the beginning, when I overturned our rented Toyota on a slippery outback road. Already in Reykjavik I had contracted Drangey fever, longing for that island where Grettir had lived out his last years and died because of an old woman's rune magic, and I had telephoned around the north of Iceland in search of someone who could transport us there.

All phone calls led to Jon Eiriksson, the farmer at Fagranes, the last farm before Reykir on the shores of Skagafjord. He had a boat in which he would take groups large enough to be worth his trouble on a day trip to Drangey. "But I want to stay there overnight," I protested in my meager Icelandic, for he knew almost no English. "Impossible," said his voice on the phone. With such impediment, perversely, my desire grew.

As I write this I have just been reading in the *Scientific American* about our most ancient Mother, called Eve by molecular biologists because she is the mitochondrial DNA-traced mother of all of us. Those who oppose the theory that our first mother is a particular human woman, of some two hundred thousand years ago, instead trace us back twice as far to a single African "apewoman" from whom humanity developed multiregionally (simultaneously in a number of different regions). But even they propose one maternal ancestor for everyone, tracing our heritage through our mothers and agreeing that we are all closely related. Perhaps she whom I have called the Goddess is that primordial "Eve," whether human or apewoman, standing up on the veldt and sparking our blood with a lust for horizons.

Yet this peculiar urge of mine to be freely alone in a special place is a feature not of my mother's line but of my father's: his family transmits the hermit gene. Before I was born, my father's brother had left society to "live off the land" in the Carolinas, becoming what is disparagingly called there a swamp rat; he caught the biggest alligator ever taken alive and sold it to the Bronx Zoo—at least that is how I remember the story. My brother is an astronomer, living alone at a mountaintop observatory. My father used to escape up the California mountains behind our house, carrying me in a homemade papoose pack before I could walk. Finally he gave up being a respectable CPA and opened a tufa mine in the high desert, living there alone and content under all that sky. But first, for good or ill, he gave me this legacy: once I could walk in the mountains on my own two feet, "Take long strides," he would say, "don't mince." My girlfriends in school, whose opinions at the time far outvalued my father's, thought I walked funny. "Your steps are too big. You don't swing your hips right. Marijane, you're walking like a *boy!*" You can't please everyone. Goddess, what shall I do?

I want to stride out alone, long steps and free, to walk like myself over the flat top of Drangey.

In Reykjavik, on the phone, I agreed with farmer Jon that it would be practical for Gillian and me to stay in his accommodations, he and I both being fully aware that this would place us nose to nose for further negotiations about the trip to the island. After rolling our car over and enduring the delays thereby incurred, Gillian and I finally made it to the north of Iceland, and drove past the town Saudarkrokur up the unpaved shoreline road on the west side of Skagafjord, going farther north. At the foot of craggy Tindastoll, a mountain haunted, the story says, by the troll king and his daughter, is the farm called Fagranes, owned by Jon Eiriksson. He was not there when we arrived. His daughter showed us to the long upstairs room reserved for travelers, where we had provisionally booked reservations, and we hated it. There was no place to cook, no desk to write on, and—well, we just hated it. It wouldn't do, we explained. Hmm. There *is* the old farmhouse, suggested the farmer's daughter.

This little farmhouse was set off from the bigger, newer one by a few hundred yards, across a farm track and a stream. We went to see it. I liked the concrete and stone front stoop where one could sit and look out over the fjord, keeping an eye on Drangey. But I hated the dead flies and the few live ones that were bumping against the windowpanes. (Icelandic summer flies are the size of bumblebees.) Gillian adored the privacy and the kitchen equipped with all the pots and pans she could wish for, battered though they were. We can get rid of the flies, said the farmer's two daughters, another having arrived. So while Gillian and I went to town for supplies, they cleaned the house for us, and we settled in happily for our stay, each with a large room to herself, sheer luxury. (No flies.) We sat on the stoop and watched the colors of the sunset streak the fjord on this serenely quiet evening, then made a big dinner of something that Gillian would no doubt remember in detail. I only remember how delicious it tasted to us, weary as we were, and how comfortable we became, nesting in. Our world was now bounded by the bulk of Tindastoll behind us, the town Saudarkrokur some miles south, a remote farm to our north (we saw cars going to and fro), and the smooth fjord shining like a shield, with Drangey a distant shadow. The hills on the other side of the fjord were still a pale blue in the twilight.

"The extent of each region," says Elisabeth Ströker, "is relative to a project and to the possibilities of activity to be realized in it. Regions as such are not first established and opened but rather arise with what is encountered in them. What is encountered determines the extent and the limitation of regions, including their further articulation and the eventual possibility of 'nesting' of domains and thereby the *structuration* of space" (1987: 55, her emphasis). She gives the example of the sea, a single homogeneous region confronting a wanderer as impassable, "while the fisherman, the swimmer, and the seafarer, in their differently motivated actions, know how to discern its various regions; for them it is structured differently" (55). On our first night at Fagranes, as I took one last look out over the darkening fjord, it appeared smooth enough to walk on, a long six- or seven-mile walk, I would estimate, from this farm to the island. But if Drangey were that easy of access it would have no attraction; Grettir would never have been advised to go there, nor would I have been seized with desire. Grettir, needing to rekindle the fire that his careless servant had let go out, had to swim four miles of icy sea from the island to the nearest point of land, and that shore he swam to was the Reykir headland some miles north from us (see plate 13). For us wanderers driven by less than life-and-death need, the sea was impassable without a boat; we were dependent entirely on Jon's good will. We would meet him tomorrow, for he had been away from the farm today. The troll-haunted mountain loomed behind our house, a boundary of no interest—even when we sat at the kitchen table facing it through the window. Our attention was focused out through the front door, across the fjord.

The glassy seas of evening were obliterated the next morning; the weather was cold and the fjord choppy. We waited around but nobody came to tell us what was happening or what to hope for, so finally we went to the main house and knocked tentatively on the front door. No, Jon was not available today, and in any case the weather was not good for crossing to Drangey. Perhaps tomorrow.

Frustrated, we went shopping, ostensibly for food. It turned out there was a sale on in Saudarkrokur, so Gillian the horsewoman bought white riding gloves but *not* the perfect but outrageously expensive tweed jacket that she tried on, and I bought, in that cold town on the north edge of Iceland, a pair of black silk shorts to wear with sandals in California. Feeling refreshed, we purchased the necessaries for a feast, went home to cook and relish it, and waited some more. The wind began to howl, trolls from the mountain, Grettir's ghost.

When Grettir won his fight against Glam in the Dale of Shadows, the troll fell backward across the threshold of the farmhouse and his eyes glared up at the moon. "You will always see before you these eyes of mine," he proclaimed, "and they will make your solitude unbearable, and this shall drag you to your death." As soon as Glam had spoken these words, the saga continues, "the faintness that had come over Grettir left him. He drew his short sword, cut off Glam's head, and placed it against his buttocks" (chapter 35). This fight took place before Grettir had been outlawed, and his fear of being alone in the dark, Glam's legacy, indeed proved a terrible disability for him later. But he had his brother Illugi to keep him company on the island in those last days, as well as his negligent servant Glaum—whose name is so much like Glam's that one must wonder. It was Glaum who finally opened the way to Grettir's foes: he left them a way of access by forgetting to draw the rope ladder up the cliff face. To this day, except for the most sure-footed, suction-fingered mountaineer, the island fortress is impenetrable without the ladder. Even more so without a boat, I thought morosely.

And now, worse luck, a storm was brewing. The wind was whipping around the house. Night fell early, dark as doom.

The next morning was wet and blowy as we both sat irritably in the kitchen, trying to read. There came a knock at the door. We were invited for coffee; would we care to come over in a half hour? Delighted! Anything to get out of the house. Combed, freshened, in a far better mood—even though we arrived wet and windblown—we went visiting at Jon's house, finally to meet him and his wife and to be regaled with cake and the strong coffee Icelanders love, followed by a professionally made video of Drangey. The video was very long, featuring Jon as hero and showing the local farmers gathering eggs from the cliffs. Despite the heavily dramatic score, seagulls wheeling to the strains of Tchaikovsky, I quite liked watching the egg-gatherers dangle by perilous ropes to cling to the wet black rocks with the sea growling far below. We saw the island presented as a fortress of rock, the unscalable glass mountain of fairy tale. It was black and slippery, with flying buttresses of lava thrust straight up from the sea bottom. We saw in the film a little hut on the grassy plateau on top of the island, old-fashioned with its crossed gable timbers and turf roof, where the egg-gatherers cooked their meals and slept dry from the spring rains.

"So you want to go to Drangey," said Jon, as though this were a sudden whim that had just now taken my fancy.

"Yes," I replied. "I want to sleep there, alone."

"Impossible. You might walk off the cliff. Dangerous. Besides, you saw what the seas were like today. Perhaps I could not come back for you for days."

"I can be ready for that."

He shook his head. I steeled my resolution.

The next day the seas were still choppy but bright, flashing beams everywhere. Gillian and I sat out on our little sheltered stoop, basking and waiting, watching the activities on the farm just south of us. Hours passed and the wind abated. Jon was doing something with a tractor as his sons and daughters came and went in various vehicles. Finally Gillian said, "Do you really want to go to Drangey?"

"Yes, of course," I replied.

"Then do something."

"What?"

She was becoming quite frustrated by the inaction. "He's just playing games with us! Go lay it on the line. Offer him money, lots of it."

"*That* would blow it," I grumbled. But I sauntered off down the hill, over the stream, up to Jon and his tractor. He was fixing it, a farmer fixing his tractor, doing what he must. I sat on a block of wood and watched, chewing a grass stem. He pulled out a broken spoke, so we went into the barn, which contained a workshop, and I stood to one side as he took another machine apart, sawing off a piece of rod to the length he needed and soldering it into shape. "One makes do with what one's got," he said in Icelandic.

We went outside again. "My father used to say that," I commented truthfully, leaning against the piece he was wedging, lending my weight. The part clicked into place and he stood back, satisfied.

Grinning, he challenged me. "You want to meet the ghost of Grettir."

"Yes," I said. But really it was the island I wanted.

His wife came to the back window of the farmhouse, calling him to lunch. "Maybe the weather will be better now," said Jon. "We will see."

I went back over the stream and up the hill to our little white house, where Gillian was waiting. "You were there an awfully long time," she said crossly. "What was all that about?"

"He was fixing his tractor," I said. "I think he'll take us now."

"How much did you offer him?"

"Nothing. We'll just pay what everyone does. I talked about my father."

She regarded me with admiration. "You really are a schemer."

"No, I'm not. I was just doing it his way. Like a dance."

She shrugged. "Rather a slow one. *I* think you're both just playing games."

But this most feisty and engaging of Brits then said, "Let's go and eat in Saudarkrokur. Since it's a fishing village, we can probably get some good fresh fish." What I want to know is, how can she think so unceasingly of food, and stay slim?

We got hot dogs, good Icelandic ones, and I bought several loaves of the excellent local bread, just in case. Bread and fresh water are all the food that one needs to survive for a few days, not that I really expected to be stranded more than overnight. When we got home, Jon's daughter Ásta came to tell us to be ready in an hour. So we packed our dinner of sandwiches, Gillian checked her camera, and I stuffed my sleeping bag and a few other essentials into my backpack, with the loaves on top. Then I thought to put in an extra wool sweater and cap, some more socks, and *Grettir's Saga*. I added a flashlight, but then, considering the brevity of the summer night, decided that the weight wasn't worth it, and jettisoned it. I put in my toothbrush and comb, my Swiss army knife, an orange, a pack of rye crisps, some bouillon cubes, caviar in a tube, tea bags, and matches in their waterproof container. Always be prepared. When Jon and Ásta came to drive with us to Saudarkrokur, where the boat was moored, I showed him how prepared I was. He smiled. I guessed then that, amused but also impressed by the seriousness of my purpose, he had succumbed and I would get to stay on Drangey. So I dashed back and grabbed my American pillowcase for a touch of luxury. Fresh water and bread (with a bit of caviar), a 200-threads-per-square-inch Egyptian cotton case to stuff my jacket into for a pillow, and warmth and shelter. What more does one need?

At the wharf in Saudarkrokur other passengers were waiting, women and children. We set off across the fjord, and after nearly an hour, the island coming constantly, enticingly, closer, we came into its high shadow to anchor in a small sheltered bay. There was a handkerchief-sized beach for landing the rubber raft that took us ashore. Then up the path, sometimes only a boot's-width above a sheer drop (yes, that scared me!), and on up the wearisome ladders, steel ones anchored into the rock that replaced the rope ladders of Grettir's day. The children, about whom I had been concerned, went up like mountain sheep, and Jon's teenage daughter Ásta practically levitated. Jon, whose game, thank goodness, was now gallantry, carried my heavy pack, while I in turn toted Gillian's cumbersome camera bag. I thought I would die of exhaustion before we reached the top, and expected that arriving there would certainly be a letdown after all the wishing and effort. Fulfilled wishes so rarely fulfill. But I didn't die and arriving was no letdown. The top of the island was covered in incredibly lush turf, with the egg-gatherers' hut protected in a bowl-shaped flowery meadow. When we flung ourselves down on the grass, the scent of crushed thyme filled the sunny air. It was heaven. If God was normally up beyond the stars, he had touched down here rather recently.

Not God, explained Jon, but bird droppings. The top of Drangey is a grassy heaven because of the guano that fertilizes and even helps create the soil. It is one of the richest soils on earth. Now I understood why the farmers of Grettir's day kept sheep up here in this nearly inaccessible meadowland, those sheep that Grettir and his companions snatched to supplement with meat and milk the fish-and-egg diet that sustained them for two long years. How those farmers hauled their flocks up and down the cliffs was another question. Jon and I walked along the one path of the island, shoulders touching companionably. "This is Jon's Street, Jónsvegur," he confided, naming it after himself. "I'll get a sign made," I laughed, "so that no one can doubt it."

On our tour of the island, Jon showed us the hole in the turf that was supposed to mark the site of Grettir's house, or maybe his lookout point. A semiprotected spot from which one could see down most of the length of the fjord, there was scarcely room inside for a single person to sit in comfort. Of course it bore no resemblance to what might have been there a thousand years ago, if indeed this hole had anything to do with Grettir at all.

Jon also showed us where the freshwater spring was, and again, in a thousand years, the water could well have shifted its course. But now I felt faint as I looked down where he pointed, and thought that if I had to survive on that water provided by nature, instead of what we brought along with us in bottles, I couldn't. I would die. I would die before I even considered negotiating the way down to it, I decided, perhaps underrating my own survival instincts. To get to this spring one had to swing out on a rope over a cliff that dropped several hundred feet to the hungry waves below, to land on a tiny outward-sloping ledge, slippery with the long grass and moss that grew beneath the freshwater trickle. Forget it. I could hardly look at that ledge. So much for my solitary paradisal island. I would need a man Friday, with less vertigo and stronger rope arms than I had, just to keep me from getting thirsty.

We marched back up to the top of the island for our picnic lunches. With a sigh I popped open my can of mineral water. "What's wrong?" asked the little girl by my side. I could not have expressed it adequately in English, much less in Icelandic, so I just offered her a mint, holding out the candy bag for her to deposit the wrapper. I would not leave my twentieth-century rubbish around for the ghost of Grettir to mourn over. But then I had to smile at the misplaced environmental correctness of my fantasy, for Grettir in his survival situation would have cherished a bit of our trash. I imagined the three companions scrabbling through the contents of my backpack, mint wrappers and all, if I could tip it out into their sparsely provisioned eleventh-century hut: "Illugi, old chap, how about a spot of caviar on your rye crisp?" And here I had packed these supplies with the thought of playing castaway for a mere two or three days, no more. "Have another," I invited my young friend, wishing that I could thrust my bag through the barrier of time to offer a mint to Grettir.

Would he be sitting near enough to hand them to, or would I have to get up and walk over to him? What are we doing, anyway, following in

113

Figure 22. The stone at Bjarg beneath which Grettir's head may be buried.

the steps of a semifictional character as if he had really been there in the flesh in those places associated with him? In fact, how fictional is Grettir? Two years ago a young pastor took Gillian and me to Grettir's birthplace, the farm Bjarg in Middale, and introduced us to the farmer who lives there. He indicated the stone, now designated a national monument in the deeds to the farm, that marks the spot where Grettir's mother is supposed to have had his head buried, his slayers having brought it to her to prove that the outlaw was truly dead—and perhaps to prevent the avenging corpse from walking by keeping the head away from the body, an ancient precaution. We asked the two men whether they believed that Grettir's head really lay buried beneath that stone (see figure 22). They affirmed that they did. This of course proves nothing, but it made us *feel* in touch with a certain reality, a time long past that the people around us believed in. In following the movements of Grettir the Outlaw we may be following only those of the saga writer, going to places that he knew and evoked for his story, or we may be going to sites known to others who earlier invented parts of Grettir's story. Perhaps the saga writer never got to Drangey; because it is difficult of access, the chances are good that he did not. Or perhaps there was an actual outlaw named Grettir who sought refuge here with his brother and a servant.

There is absolutely no way of retrieving the truth of this matter without more information than we have now or are ever likely to have. Nevertheless, being in touch with these real sites, with the terrains or shapes of land that the saga characters confronted, places us who are here now in an intimate relationship with those who were here then. Grettir slept here and I shall too. Even if he does sit too far away now for me to offer him a mint. The issue of his fictionality is secondary, irrelevant.

Why do I think of Grettir mostly in shadow? Perhaps it has something to do with his fear of the dark. In any case, as I sit here writing this essay while it is raining in California, imagining myself back on that sunny island handing around the mints, I see Grettir's face against the darkness, illuminated by firelight. No, I wouldn't recognize him on the street, but I think he looks a bit like the German actor Klaus Maria Brandauer, only larger and bulkier.

That evening I did experience the island in darkness. As I had hoped they would, the Icelanders and Gillian left me there, thinking I was crazy. Gillian was looking forward to renting a horse, in my absence, and riding north along the coast to Reykir, the farm Grettir swam to for fire. She hoped to find the hot spring where he had soaked out his soreness. Jon's youngest son and his best friend would ride along with her. And I would be on Drangey alone. I couldn't believe how contented I was as I watched the boat growing smaller in the distance, heard the sound of its motor diminishing, until there was only the cry of the seabirds, and two ravens, the island pair, who came out to peer at me now and then and flew away squawking. I was wholly alone, much more alone than most of us in modern civilization ever get a chance to be, and "safe as houses," as the expression goes, except that no house these days is so safe from intruders as Drangey. Marooned, I was ecstatic. Marooned. I repeated the word a few times like a spell, a caress. I crooned it: "Marooned, marooned." The day was still warm, and I flew around the island like a person deranged, throwing my arms out, rolling in that delicious warm grass, jumping up and running again, then just taking my long strides, walking like myself. Finally, exhausted, I settled down to enjoy my stay, hoping for stormy weather to prolong it. But could I *really* imagine stormy weather?

I got out one of my loaves and tore off a piece, sprinkling it with bits of just-plucked wild thyme. Castaway-fare in hand, I strolled down to the far end of the island and sat on the edge of the lookout hollow, to think myself into Grettir's frame of mind while nibbling my morsel. But I couldn't. With everyone else gone, so was Grettir, and besides, he was dead, his head lying under that faraway stone at Bjarg. I was truly alone. No ghosts, only ravens.

I did not tire of it. "The corporeal being located at the periphery of space has become a *subject*," says Elisabeth Ströker, not meaning quite what I mean by her words or her emphasis. "[S]he finds [her]self in a position of absolute opposition to the world" (1987: 93). As I lay against the grass on my blue mac, a small plane flew by overhead, and I wondered what they thought of a person on the island without a boat bobbing in the bay below, a person marooned. Who cares, I thought, so long as I don't get "rescued." I felt intruded on by them above, made an object again by the thought of their eyeing me, but the plane was my object, too. I walked back to the hollow where the hut was, and the plane circled and flew away. Then there was nothing to watch but the long changing of the colors of the sky at sunset, out over the fjord. The isolation of being here on Grettir's island, without Grettir, was like a word I had long been searching for. Grettir was somehow in touch with this isolation, understanding it. His very fear of it reveals his awareness. Right now I was more in touch with Grettir than with anyone else, but he wasn't here, only the word was, the word that he knew too and that cannot be said because it only exists at the periphery where there is no one to say it to. In a letter to Constance Malleson written in 1918, Bertrand Russell says:

> I *must*, before I die, find *some* way to say the essential thing that is in me, that I have never said yet—a thing that is not love or hate or pity or scorn, but the very breath of life, fierce and coming from far away, bringing into human life the vastness and fearful passionless force of non-human things. (1967: 116)

Finally the sun went down and the chill in the air drove me into the little hut. I lit the kerosene lamp in the way Jon had taught me, and lit the stove, and made a cup of broth. Then I spent quite a long time composing a poem on a paper towel and copying it in the guest book, something about not finding Grettir on Drangey. I didn't say "thank goodness"; that would have been rude. It was by now very late and I was more sleepy than hungry, so I blew out the lamp and damped the stove, and got into my sleeping bag, expecting to wake up early to a long, leisurely morning on the sunlit island before the boat could possibly come back for me. The furnishings were primitive, foam mattresses on boards, but more comfortable than camping out. I slept like a log. Surely, on this edge of nonhuman vastness, I was as safe as I had ever been. No one was on the island but me. Even my dreams were deserted.

The next morning, lying chilled despite extra socks and sweater and cap, I woke to the sound of rain. It was surprisingly late. I got up, tried rather feebly to stoke the fire from the night before, got enough heat to boil water but not much more, and had another hot cup of broth, dipping bread into it, one of my favorite things. Even when the rain stopped, it was so cold! I went outside, and it was cold out there too, and gray, and I was an excessively corporeal being at the periphery of space, whose opposing world had floated away in the night. The seabirds themselves were subdued. Clouds hung heavy all around the island. Well, nobody was going to come for me in this weather. So I went inside and crawled into my sleeping bag, reaching for *Grettir's Saga.* I had been rereading it, and was up to the fight with Glam. I had forgotten that he was a Swedish laborer, a thrall who had been slain in a struggle with a supernatural being and whose body that being had taken over. He returns to prey on the farms he was familiar with when he was alive, and no one dares face him until Grettir takes on the task. In the dim light from the dim day that filtered into the hut, I read on, growing sleepier as I read. Grettir comes to take on Glam partly out of interest, partly to test his own enormous strength. Normally I would feel funny dozing off at 11:00 A.M., improper. In our culture this is not allowed. Afternoon naps are occasionally permitted, but never late-morning ones. But opposition was elsewhere, I could do what I liked. Feeling drugged with the need for sleep, I could hardly keep my eyes open. I came to the point where "the door was opened, and Grettir saw the thrall stretching his head through it, and the head was hideously huge, with enormous features." But I had read the story, I knew what would happen next. I let the book drop from my hands and fell asleep, and again I did not dream of anyone. I was alone on the island.

Or so I had assumed. A series of squishing footfalls outside the hut shocked me awake. There *can't* be anyone, I thought. If it had been night and there were time enough to think about it, I would have been terrified. But as I looked up, half expecting a huge-headed specter (or Grettir, headless), the door burst open, and there, dripping wet in the glaring brightness, stood Ásta, risen from the sea. "Hurry," she panted, "the boat's waiting."

We threw things into my pack, leaving the tube of caviar for the next visitors to the hut. Ásta grabbed the uneaten loaves in their plastic bag, and we ran and slid and shimmied down the track to the bay. Actually, once past the ladders, we mostly skreed. Those who have done it will know what I mean: you skate down the loose rubble of the mountainside, going from side to side to avoid gaining so much speed that you tumble.

At one point, to avoid the narrowness of the track, I took a wrong turn that went nowhere, except to a hollowed-out nesting hole in the rock, where I came eye to eye with an eiderdown duck. On this island suddenly of eyes both it and I were pretty startled, jerked suddenly into subjecthood and objecthood. Then I got back on track, and scrambled down to where Ásta was waiting at the rubber raft. With difficulty because the sea was so choppy, I threw my gear and myself into the raft and she pushed us off, her father reeling us out to his fishing boat with a rope.

"What's wrong with the motor?" I asked as we were being pulled along.

"It isn't working," Ásta explained. "I had to swim to shore with the rope, then pull the raft after me."

I guess the ghost of Grettir was present after all. No normal human being would enter that ice-cold sea.

Except that I don't believe in ghosts, at least not in Grettir's case. He simply was not there on Drangey. "No," I reported to Jon, who asked. "I didn't see him." And Ásta was simply one of those crazy Icelanders who think they can do anything, and often can. After changing out of her wet clothes in the cabin, she wrapped herself in a woollen blanket (see plate 14). Shivering and hunched, she seemed like a hybrid of waif and wild native, but pale as a corpse, and headless as she ducked inside her cocoon for warmth. After a while her color came back and she emerged. She came out on deck and stood by the rail, letting her hair blow out in the wind. The boat slapped across the waves, returning.

Drangey receded in the distance as the sun came out. It remained an island of mystery, desirable, unattainable—except that I had been there. I slept alone there, undreaming on the edge of the world. Now my trace must still be there, mingling with that of those others, whispering the word in the grasses in the wild weather. Thinking of that, I am absent from myself *here*, wherever this is. I am both in and absent from my place, like Grettir, and there is light, and a strangely satisfying attunement with otherness. Also a lingering desire.

Notes

Introduction

1. We are using Paul Ricoeur's classifications here as he outlines them in *The Reality of the Historical Past* and as these are discussed by archaeologist Julian Thomas in "Same, Other, Analogue: Writing the Past," in *Writing the Past in the Present*, ed. Frederick Baker and Julian Thomas, 18–23.

2. See also *Desire for Origins: New Language, Old English, and Teaching the Tradition*, where Frantzen gives a comprehensive overview of the history of Anglo-Saxon scholarship, deconstructing the "neutrality" of the tradition and analyzing the ways in which critical ideology has shaped the discipline. Frantzen's influential work considerably develops the debate in medieval studies about the nature of the role of the critic and the integration, both historical and personal, of that role. Earlier work, such as Lee Patterson's *Negotiating the Past: The Historical Understanding of Medieval Literature*, cleared ground for such a dialogue, although caught in the early constraints of the debate by virtue of its oppositional construction of past and present. Patterson introduces, but does not fully theorize, the possibilities of "negotiation." Gillian R. Overing also argues for self-conscious attention to critical practice in *Language, Sign and Gender in Beowulf* and in "Recent Writing on Old English: A Response,"in *Æstel*, where she discusses current critical developments.

3. Although the term "negotiation" may resonate with Patterson's *Negotiating the Past*, it is used here with a somewhat different and more extended focus, in order to describe the activity and process of scholarly investigation more fully *as* activity and process. See note 2 of this Introduction, and especially the discussion in chapter 2 on "Places in Question."

4. The uncertainty of the location increases with modern scholarship. F. P. Magoun (1953) was able to locate this battle so exactly as to provide an itinerary, and Godfrid Storms (1970) argued for a different but equally precise date as well as location, but Walter Goffart's recent discussion puts both of the preceding in doubt, pointing out that the eighth-century account upon whose details these scholars base their findings "contains many freely added geographical details" not in the earlier and probably more precise narrative of Gregory of Tours (1981: 86).

1. Mapping *Beowulf*

The first section of this chapter, "Reinventing Beowulf's Voyage to Denmark," was written by Gillian; the second section, "Traveling Home with Beowulf," was written by Marijane. Marijane is grateful to Professor T. A. Shippey for helpful comments throughout her section.

1. Arguments for the identification of the Geats with the historical Gautar can be found in R. W. Chambers (1963) and R. T. Farrell (1972). A good, if biased, summary of opposing arguments can be found in Viggo Starcke (1962).

Notes to Chapter 1

2. Fred C. Robinson has recently affirmed this view of the location of Heorot in his essay "Teaching the Backgrounds: History, Religion, Culture": "Much of the circumstantial detail in the poem is shown by parallel sources from the continent to be part of the legendary history of Scandinavia and not the English poet's invention. Hrothgar (and later Hrothulf) ruled from a royal settlement whose present location can with fair confidence be fixed as the modern Danish village of Leire, the actual location of Heorot" (109). For another view see Saxo Grammaticus, *A History of the Danes*, 2:46.

3. All references to *Beowulf* throughout the book are taken from Klaeber's edition. The translations are our own.

4. In choosing to base our speed and course on Ohthere's account of his voyage, we had assumed that our modern yacht would possess considerably superior navigational abilities and that we would take such differences into account. Ohthere's boat, however, would have been far more agile than we supposed. When he waited for a following wind, for example, it was usually by choice: "It would be wrong to conclude that his ship was unable to sail close to the wind. The explanation is, rather, that on entering unknown waters, Ohthere wanted as much wind room as possible for manoeuvres so that he could without difficulty avoid any unexpected obstacles that might occur. Had he attempted to reach, that is sail with the wind abeam, or to sail on the wind in waters with complex currents and with the possibility of snow showers, there was a risk that he might not be able to sail out of danger. The lines of the hull and details of the rigging of Viking ships that have so far been found show that at least the cargo-boats were designed to have a good capacity to tack against the wind" (Crumlin-Pedersen, 1984: 32). Tacking was possible, then, though in a gentle breeze it is a laborious process for any craft, Viking or modern. Ohthere would have solved this problem simply by rowing into the wind without sail, an option paralleled by our occasional use of the motor.

5. Much has been written about this passage of the poem, which has been used to support a variety of points of view different from ours, ones in which visions and descriptions of landscape are perceived as essentially derivative or formulaic. See, for example, Crowne (1960); Clark (1965); and Andersson (1976: 146–52). There are indeed striking parallels to this passage elsewhere in Old English poetry, notably Andreas's recognition of Mermedonia in *Andreas* ll.840b–841a (see Clark, 654–57). For a contrasting discussion of the dynamic effect of this passage, see Overing (1986). See also Klaeber's comments on the derivative nature of landscape descriptions in *Beowulf* (183), which are discussed further by Osborn in the next section of this chapter.

6. I am adopting the name Wedermark here to designate a nation, in a usage analogous to that of the name Denmark. The concept of nation is anachronistic in terms of the tribal society of Beowulf's sixth century (see Farrell, 1982), but perhaps not in the age of the poet. "Denemearc" appears for the first time in King Alfred's preface to the late-ninth-century translation of Orosius (see Jones, 1984: 114, note), probably echoing the usage of his informant Ohthere. Also analogous is Hugmerck, home of the Hugas, a tribe represented in *Beowulf* by Hygelac's slayer Dæghrefn (line 2502). Hugmerck, probably designating "modern Humsterland, the district around Groningen in Dutch Friesland" (Haywood, 1991: 81), first appears in the *Vita S. Luidgeri*, which is, like the Orosius, a ninth-century document (Pertz, 1829: 410; see also Haywood 180, n. 20). For a critical discussion questioning the very identity of the Hugas, see Goffart (1981: 90–100); he does not mention the place-name, and he associates the tribal name with the politics of the early tenth century (99). Snorri mentions Vingulmork, Heithmork, and so on (*Heimskringla*, 48–58, and passim). "Mark" with its variant vowels originally meant border or "margin" (which the OED suggests is cognate): a frontier. In Old Norse it sometimes designates a wooded terrain, as in the "Markland" of the Vinland Sagas, but in other names it merely means "land" or "territory." That the territory thus designated need not be extensive is suggested by, for example, the place-name "Dragsmark," which appears later in this essay. If Wedermark in *Beowulf* is intended to name a tribal territory, the fact that the only similar forms are found from the

ninth century onward may be a small item of circumstantial evidence supporting the later date for the poem proposed by numerous contributors to *The Dating of Beowulf* (Chase, 1981).

7. Though not the first to suggest the Jute hypothesis, Pontus Fahlbeck offered the first extended argument that the Geats of *Beowulf* were Jutes in his "Beovulfskvädet såsom källa för nordisk fornhistoria," summarized and critiqued in German by Sarrazin (1888: 23) and later in English by Chambers (1963: 8–9; he reviews the whole "Jute question" on 333–45 and 401–18). In Scandinavia, surprisingly, the subject "continues to be a matter for discussion among scholars, who are nowadays the only persons who retain an interest in the problem" (Henrikson, 1966: 40). Another Swedish scholar, Knut Stjerna, suggested that Öland was the homeland of the Geats in his *Essays on Questions Connected with the Old English Poem of Beowulf* (1912: 90–96), and Huppé, perhaps following Grundtvig as reported by Klaeber (1950: xlvi), has them live "in a legendary land placed somewhere in Scandinavia . . . perhaps the island of Gotland, the legendary home of the Goths" (14). An extensive argument that the Geats of *Beowulf* were an entirely mythical tribe invented by the poet, making their homeland mythical also, was published by Jane Acomb Leake in 1967.

8. I am nearly certain this is Stanley's statement, but cannot find where he says it. In his essay on the dating of *Beowulf*, he elaborates this opinion with specific reference to the poem in terms so evocative as to be worth quoting for their own sake: "The poet is remarkably good at enduing the impossible with reality. He teaches us how to strike a dragon to kill, and how, when opportunity serves, a dragon hot and fierce encompasses a warrior's neck all round, till the life-blood surges forth wave upon wave. When the fight is on in Heorot, the poet makes the meadbenches coil away from the foundation-planks with the violence of the superhuman Beowulf and the supernatural Grendel on that floor. A poet who is excellent at letting us experience what he himself cannot have seen is not to be trusted as witness. Heroic society as he presents it is real, not because he was near to it, but because he has the poetic skill so to present it" (Chase, 1981: 202). These are wise words; yet as so often is the case with Stanley, he seems rather to suggest that we shut down inquiry than that we should proceed more alertly than before.

9. The *Beowulf* poet suppresses what actually went on in such places; I refer the reader who wishes to know more to P. V. Glob's romanticized but enthralling account in *The Bog People: Iron Age Man Preserved*, with its expressive photographs that have inspired the Irish poet Seamus Heaney to some of his most moving lyrics. Glob's title is misleading, because he also writes of the corpses of women preserved in peat, my own favorite being the graceful "young girl from the Windeby bog" (plate 38). Not only on the Continent did such customs prevail, however. T. A. Shippey reminds me, for example, of "the Yorkshire burial with the old lady on the bottom, and on the top a young one, thrown in to be buried alive, with her back broken, and the heaved-in millstone that broke it still on top" (personal letter, March 25, 1993). It is intriguing to contemplate the nature and purpose of a poet who invents ancestral figures too noble for such atrocities.

10. Probably the most famous and dramatic of all literary ship funerals is that of Baldur the Fair, whose ship was fired and set adrift. It is notable that Scyld's funeral ship in *Beowulf*, though set adrift, was not set alight, and was possibly expected to come to shore somewhere in the real world, though lines 50a–52 can equally refer to the supernatural other world. Curiously, the closest real-world analogue to this "Germanic" ship funeral of which we have record was that of the Celtic saint, Gildas; see A. F. Cameron (1969). The great English ship burial about which so much has been written is that at Sutton Hoo in East Anglia; the definitive work is still R. L. S. Bruce-Mitford's three-volume account. C. L. Wrenn enthusiastically assesses its relevance to *Beowulf* in Chambers (1963: 508–23), and in an amusing, ironic essay Roberta Frank (1992) has recently reassessed these connections and the scholarly impulse to make them. For an archaeological account of the Scandinavian practice of ship burial, see Roesdahl (1992: especially 160–62). In his famous *risala*, the

ninth-century merchant Ibn Fadlan offers a fascinating Arabic perspective on the funeral obsequies of a Swedish chieftain (see Smyser, 1965).

11. This information about the Raum Älf from the *Norsk Stednavneleksikon* (unavailable to me in California) was kindly offered by Gillian Fellows Jensen and forwarded to me by Ole Crumlin-Pedersen in a letter of October 25, 1985. It confirms the information in Hollander's map between pages 6 and 7 of his translation of the *Heimskringla.*

12. The implication in *Heimskringla* (1964: 48) that the name of King Álfar is related to the place-name Alfheim reminds one of Henry B. Woolf's long-ago suggestion that the mysterious Ælfhere of line 2604 (which might be compared to Alfwalda, line 1314, which Klaeber emends) might have been Beowulf's "true" name. Earlier, in chapter 22, Snorri has made Hugleik, synonymous with Beowulf's uncle Hygelac, the son of a Swedish King Alf (*Heimskringla,* 23–25); comparison of his account with that of Saxo Grammaticus might turn up firmer associations of "Hugleik" with the area of Weder Isle Fjord.

13. Here the subject is the king who undertook the raid; more will be said later about the raid itself. The three documents outside the poem that mention this raid are Gregory of Tours's *History of the Franks* (written circa 575–594 A.D.), which makes Hygelac a Danish king; the *Liber Historia Francorum* (727 A.D.), which has him raid upon the Hetwares as in *Beowulf,* again as a Danish king (except that in one manuscript *Gotorum* appears but is crossed out; see Wadstein, 1933: 282); and the *Liber Monstrorum* (circa 800 A.D.), in which he is king of the Geats (or Goti). The relevant passages from these sources are given in the original and discussed by Chambers (1963: 3–4). It is clear that these texts derive their information sequentially from one another, but the *Liber Historia Francorum* contains details, such as the tribal name Hetuarii, found elsewhere only in *Beowulf.* Therefore Walter Goffart (1981: 87) argues that "the unanimous agreement of the poem with the eighth-century historian is difficult to explain otherwise than by supposing that the *Beowulf* poet used the *LHF* as his source for Hygelac's raid." A niggler could argue that the opposite might just as well be the case, the writer of the *Liber Historia Francorum* having borrowed details from *Beowulf.* Because I find convincing other suggestive evidence for a date for the poem later than the *LHF*'s mid-eighth-century date, I am inclined to agree with Goffart about the direction of this borrowing.

14. The historical "Hygelac" could even have been an agent king, in technical terms the assigned *princeps* of a *regnum* (Goffart, 1981: 96), like Hrani the Gautish, surrounded by his own Geatish (i.e., Gautish) kinsfolk, or merely a minor chieftain like Hnæf and his father Hoc in the Finnsburg story and *Widsith*; Tolkien suggests that Hnæf and Hoc represented "subordinate offshoots of expanding Danish power in regions not originally Scandinavian" (1982: 41). Perhaps Hygelac's kingdom represents Gautar expansion—or perhaps not. A "real" Wedergeat might have had a reason to visit Hrothgar's court apart from monster-killing, to bring not gifts but tribute; the second half of *Beowulf* emphasizes the shifting allegiances of peoples. In any case, if Hygelac's kingdom of Wedergeats is a subordinate offshoot of expanding power, the poem certainly mutes that subordination.

15. In the map titled "The Geography of *Beowulf*" in his translation of the poem, Wentworth Huyshe follows Sarrazin in locating Finna Land in Bohuslän, though he places the Heatho-Reamas west of modern Oslo and "Hygelac's Realm" south of the Göta Älv. Huyshe includes a section titled "The Scenes and Surroundings of *Beowulf*," part 6 of his introduction (xxxvii–xliv), and also discusses landscape in individual notes to the text.

16. Klaeber reports that "the military expedition of the Geats . . . against the Franks and the Frisians, it has been claimed, points to the Jutes rather than to the distant Götar" (xlvii). But if we think of Weder Isle Fjord rather than southern Sweden as the home of Hygelac's Geats, this Swedish coastline facing directly onto the Skagerrak and the North Sea is almost as convenient as Jutland for the launching of an attack upon Frisia, or for receiving the return attack anticipated in lines 2910b–21.

Klaeber is referring here to the old nationalistic controversy about the identity of Beowulf's Geats, whether they were Gautar, hence Swedish, or Jutes, hence Danish (see note 7 of this chapter). Although throughout this discussion I have assumed the majority view, that they are to be identified with the Gautar—I merely make them an outlying colony identified by their Weder Isles location—this Skagerrak coast of Sweden would also be easily accessible to a colony from northern Jutland, in this period when the sea was considered a highway rather than a barrier. From the Skagen of Jutland to Marstrand in Sweden is only a hop, not much more than the Dover crossing to France or the Stranraer crossing to Northern Ireland, and prevailing winds and tides would urge settlers in the direction of the Weder Isle Fjord. Finally, there is nothing in this material to reassure us that Beowulf's people, who according to the poem dispersed under pressure about the time of the Germanic settlement of England, had an existence outside the imagination of an English poet extremely able at amalgamating historical and quasi-historical traditions. It may be appropriate to add the reminder here that this chapter does not argue for the historicity of the Weder-Geats, only for their imagined location.

17. Chambers (1963: 408–19) discusses the Scandinavian accounts of this battle, but the most useful brief presentation of this complicated material remains that of Klaeber (xliii–xliv). An excellent longer account is Farrell (1972).

18. Hollander's index to *Heimskringla* (833) indicates that this Foss is in Norway. Although the place-name Fors, Foss, or English Force means "waterfall" and exists at many locations, both *Landnámabók* and *Heimskringla* refer to a particular Foss as a place that everyone knows about. It seems that at least one such important Foss may be identified with modern Forshälla a few kilometers southwest of Uddevalla (as on Hollander's map).

2. Geography in the Reader

The first four sections of this chapter were written by Gillian; the final section, "Places in Translation and the Metonymy of Terrain," was written by Marijane.

1. For a discussion of how and why place-names changed within the time period of the sagas, see Hastrup (1985: 176).

2. Interestingly, it may still be possible to reconstruct fairly exactly some of these extinct locations. Jack Ives, a glaciologist in the Department of Geography at the University of California at Davis, who graciously furnished us with maps, also has a keen interest in the sagas. He is currently engaged in determining the homesite of Kari Solmundarson. Kari managed to escape from the fire that destroyed his friend Njal, but his homesite has since disappeared beneath shifting glacial sands. See Ives (1991).

3. The "fact" of rape at this juncture in the text is debatable in that it is not explicitly stated. Indeed, in conference sessions some scholars have reacted very strongly against my statement that it *is* a rape, believing this to be too negative a construction of Grettir's behavior. The text describes the maid's refusal, or inability, to keep silent about or stop laughing at Grettir's meager sexual endowment; Grettir "seized her and spoke a stanza," after which "he pulled her up on the bench." In the next stanza Grettir warns "wait until I get into action, my lass." The text then tells us that "the maid kept crying out, but in the end, before they parted, she had stopped taunting him." Chapter 75 states that "a little later he [Grettir] got dressed," and we hear no more, literally or textually, of the maid.

I have been quoting from Fox and Pálsson's translation, but it is worth noting that in the Icelandic text of the original (Jónsson edition, 1936) the verbs used suggest a degree of force. For example, "greip hann til hennar" ("he laid hold of her") and "svipti hann henni upp" ("he swept her up"; *svipa* also connotes to swipe or deliver a blow). The maid's response is also pronounced: "Griðka œpði hástofum" ("the serving woman cried aloud"; *œpa* also connotes to weep or bewail).

In my view this scene and some of the reactions to it benefit from the kind of analysis Kathryn Gravdal has recently applied to the medieval lyric. In "Camouflaging Rape: The Rhetoric of Sexual Violence in the Medieval Pastourelle," she contends that the "most striking feature of the rape in the Old French pastourelle is its past acceptability and its current invisibility" (362), and calls attention to the strategies of both the poems and their critics to elide, ignore, or trivialize the fact of rape and its attendant brutality. Moreover, one pattern Gravdal isolates in the rape scenes of the pastourelle is the noise and struggle of the shepherdess followed by her submission and in several cases her gratitude (364)—a pattern that perhaps finds resonance in the maid's ceasing to mock Grettir. I am not claiming exact parallels between these genres and cultures, but I find Gravdal's examination of the "silences" of both texts and critics on the subject of rape to be persuasive and enlightening. See also Gravdal's *Ravishing Maidens: Writing Rape in Medieval French Literature and Law.*

4. See, for example, Annette Kolodny's two studies, *The Lay of the Land: Metaphor as Experience and History in American Life and Letters* and *The Land before Her: Fantasy and Experience of the American Frontiers, 1630–1860.* For a more general overview, see Janice Monk, "Approaches to the Study of Women and Landscape."

5. For a somewhat different view see Judith Jesch, *Women in the Viking Age,* 79–83; Jesch enumerates the women listed or implied in *Landnámabók* and comes up with what appears to be a more participatory image of women's role in the settlement process, although women's experience of this process remains undocumented. I think that Clover's anthropological argument, "The Politics of Scarcity: Notes on the Sex Ratio in Early Scandinavia," to which I refer later in this chapter, has more explanatory power in that she discusses a pansocial masculine frontier ethic and offers convincing evidence for an imbalanced sex ratio.

6. For an overview of this debate see the essays by SueEllen Campbell (1989); Jim Cheney (1987); and Michael Zimmerman (1987).

7. Grettir really seems to be in a double bind here. The idea of vagrancy, of *not being somewhere,* was socially and legally condemned: "If a man moves about on pointless journeys within a Quarter for half a month or more, the penalty for it is a fine. . . . If a man moves about and accepts charity for half a month or more and takes night lodgings where he can get them, he is a vagrant. If a man turns into a tramp—a healthy man and so ablebodied that he could get lodging for a whole year if he would do the work he is capable of— his penalty is full outlawry" (*Laws of Early Iceland: Grágás,* 1980: 135).

8.That Grettir is a study in contradiction is by no means a new observation about the hero. See Hastrup (1986), especially page 284. Hastrup sees Grettir as a "boundary" figure, mediating between human and nonhuman worlds, and also as a "joker": "Like any joker, Grettir assumes a variety of shapes according to circumstances; at the same time, however, he also remains the same" (294). Hastrup's analysis is geared to contextualizing the hero within historical and ongoing cultural tradition; she argues powerfully for the continuity of the *idea* of Grettir and its continued presence in Iceland today.

9. In her forthcoming work *Long Echoes: Old Norse Myths in Medieval Icelandic Society,* Margaret Clunies Ross seeks to reexamine the oppositional terms and attenuate the binarism of past structuralist analyses of the Old Norse mythological world. She reviews the oppositional pairs nature and culture, female and male, order and disorder, and examines aspects of the social organization of mythic or supernatural beings. I thank her for the opportunity to read the second chapter of her manuscript in progress, where she argues that we must revise and extend our classification systems in order to begin to address the complexity of the Old Norse mythic world. This certainly holds true for a figure like Grettir, who is in and out, of and not of a variety of social and supernatural spaces, a boundary figure who confuses categories.

10. See, for example, Theodore Andersson (1976) and Paul Piehler (1971).

11. For an overview of this debate, see Carol J. Clover (1985). Clover (1990: 127) offers further insight into the much-discussed "gap" between when the sagas were historically located and when they were actually written down.

12. It is very difficult to do more than hypothesize levels of volition or coercion in this instance. What *were* Gudrun's choices? Jesch points out that it was virtually unheard of in

the world of the sagas that women should make such a voyage (1991: 197), but elsewhere in her wide-ranging multidisciplinary study she offers evidence of women who traveled and traded in the Viking Age (35–37). The sagas, moreover, offer us a poor insight into women's reality; as "cultural products," Jesch argues, "they cannot be used as factual evidence about women's lives because they are the products of a predominantly masculine discourse throughout most of the Viking Age" (206). This view of the sagas' relation to women's reality is similar to Jochens's in "The Medieval Icelandic Heroine: Fact or Fiction?" where women's legal, historical, and literary positions are comparatively evaluated. Jesch chooses not to include legal sources in *Women in the Viking Age*, believing that these too are compromised and misleading sources (5). Jesch extends the overall saga debate (see note 11 of this chapter) by including many other kinds of information about women's lives and deaths, although an abundance of questions and contradictions still remains about the degree, if any, of women's choices.

13. These women, interestingly, are part of the settlement process, an area in which Jesch contends women's roles saw some expansion (1991: 79–83); they are thus perhaps more consonant with the saga image. The saga records of the achievements of Unn, for example, "however romanticised, preserve a true picture of the possibilities opened up for women in the upheaval of the viking movements" (83). For a different view of women's role in the settlement process, see Clover (1990).

14. When our manuscript was reviewed for publication, two of the three readers wanted us to incorporate some practical details about getting to the sites we visited. We are happy to say that Marijane has written a book offering just such advice regarding the Icelandic sites, *A Journey in Sagaland*, under consideration by a publisher in Reykjavik.

3. The Saga of the Saga

The first section of this chapter, "The Road to Drangey," was written by Gillian; the section "Where's Grettir?" was written by Marijane.

Works Cited

Andersson, Theodore. *Early Epic Scenery.* Ithaca: Cornell University Press, 1976.

Appleton, Jay. *The Experience of Landscape.* London: John Wiley and Sons, 1975.

Asser. "Life of King Alfred." In *Alfred the Great.* Trans. Simon Keynes and Michael Lapidge. Harmondsworth: Penguin, 1983.

Bachelard, Gaston. *The Poetics of Space.* Trans. Maria Jolas. Boston: Beacon Press, 1969. Originally published as *La Poétique de l'espace,* 1958.

Baker, Frederick, and Julian Thomas, eds. *Writing the Past in the Present.* Lampeter: Saint David's University, 1990.

Barr, Roseanne. "An Evening with Roseanne Barr." HBO: 1986.

Basso, Keith H. *Western Apache Language and Culture: Essays in Linguistic Anthropology.* Tucson: University of Arizona Press, 1990.

Bateson, Gregory. *Mind and Nature: A Necessary Unity.* New York: Bantam, 1979.

Beck, Horace. *Folklore of the Sea.* Middletown, Conn.: Wesleyan University Press, 1973.

Bede. *Bede's Ecclesiastical History of the English People.* Ed. Bertram Colgrave and R. A. B. Mynors. Oxford: Clarendon Press, 1969.

Beowulf and the Fight at Finnsburg. Ed. Fr. Klaeber. Boston: D. C. Heath, 1950.

Bertilsson, Ulf. *The Rock Carvings of Northern Bohuslän: Spatial Structures and Symbols.* Stockholm Studies in Archaeology 7. Stockholm: University of Stockholm Archaeology Department, 1987.

The Book of Settlements: Landnámabók. Trans. Hermann Pálsson and Paul Edwards. Winnipeg: University of Manitoba Press, 1972.

Bourdieu, Pierre. *Outline of a Theory of Practice.* Cambridge: Cambridge University Press, 1977.

Bruce-Mitford, R. L. S., et al. *The Sutton Hoo Ship Burial.* 3 vols. London: British Museum Publications, 1975–83.

Byock, Jesse L. *Medieval Iceland: Society, Sagas and Power.* Berkeley: University of California Press, 1988.

———. "Saga Form, Oral History, and the Icelandic Social Context." *New Literary History* 16, no. 1 (1984–85): 153–73.

Cameron, A. F. "Saint Gildas and Scyld Scefing." *Neuphilologische Mitteilungen* 70 (1969): 240–46.

Campbell, Mary B. *The Witness and the Other World: Exotic European Travel Writing, 400–1600.* Ithaca: Cornell University Press, 1988.

Campbell, SueEllen. "The Land and Language of Desire: Where Deep Ecology and Post-Structuralism Meet." *Western American Literature* 24, no. 3 (November 1989): 199–211.

Chambers, R. W. *Beowulf: An Introduction.* 3d ed. Supplement by C. L. Wrenn. Cambridge: Cambridge University Press, 1963.

Chase, Colin, ed. *The Dating of Beowulf.* Toronto: University of Toronto Press, 1981.

Cheney, Jim. "Eco-Feminism and Deep Ecology." *Environmental Ethics* 9 (Summer 1987): 115–45.

Works Cited

Christensen, Tom. "Lejrehallen." *Skalk* 3 (1987): 4–9.

Cixous, Hélène, and Catherine Clément. *The Newly Born Woman.* Trans. Betsy Wing. Minneapolis: University of Minnesota Press, 1986.

Clark, George. "The Traveller Recognizes His Goal: A Theme in Anglo-Saxon Poetry." *Journal of English and Germanic Philology* 62 (1965): 645–59.

Clifford, James, and George E. Marcus, eds. *Writing Culture: The Poetics and Politics of Ethnography.* Berkeley: University of California Press, 1986.

Clover, Carol J. "The Politics of Scarcity: Notes on the Sex Ratio in Early Scandinavia." In *New Readings on Women in Old English Literature.* Ed. Helen Damico and Alexandra Hennessey Olsen. Bloomington: Indiana University Press, 1990. 100–134.

———. "Icelandic Family Sagas." In *Old Norse-Old Icelandic Literature: A Critical Guide.* Ed. Carol J. Clover and John Lindow. Ithaca: Cornell University Press, 1985. 239–315.

Collingwood, W. G., and Jón Stefánsson. *A Pilgrimage to the Saga-Steads of Iceland.* Ulverston: W. Holmes, 1899.

Cosijn, P. J. *Notes on Beowulf.* Leeds Texts and Monographs, n.s. 12. Leeds, England: School of English, University of Leeds, 1991. [Originally published Leiden, 1892.]

Craig, David. *Native Stones: A Book about Climbing.* London: Secker and Warburg, 1987.

Crowne, David. "The Hero on the Beach." *Neuphilologische Mitteilungen* 61 (1960): 362–72.

Crumlin-Pedersen, Ole. "Ships, Navigation and Routes in the Reports of Ohthere and Wulfstan." In *Two Voyagers at the Court of King Alfred.* Ed. Niels Lund. Trans. Christine E. Fell. York: William Sessions, Ltd., 1984. 30–42.

Damico, Helen. "Dystopic Conditions of the Mind: Toward a Study of Landscape in *Grettissaga.*" In *Geardagum* 7 (September 1986): 1–15.

Daniels, Stephen, and Dennis Cosgrove, eds. *The Iconography of Landscape.* Cambridge: Cambridge University Press, 1988. Introduction, 1–10.

de Certeau, Michel. *The Practice of Everyday Life.* Trans. Stephen Rendall. Berkeley: University of California Press, 1984.

Egil's Saga. See Snorri Sturluson.

Ekwall, Eilert. *The Concise Oxford Dictionary of English Place-Names.* 4th ed. Oxford: Clarendon, 1960.

Entrikin, J. Nicholas. *The Betweenness of Place.* London: MacMillan, 1991.

Fahlbeck, Pontus Erlend. "Beovulfskvädet såsom källa för nordisk fornhistoria." *Antikvarisk Tidskrift för Sverige* 8, no. 2 (1884): 1–88.

Farrell, Robert T. "*Beowulf* and the Northern Heroic Age." In *The Vikings.* Ed. R. T. Farrell. London: Phillimore, 1982. 180–216.

———. "*Beowulf,* Swedes, and Geats." *Saga-Book of the Viking Society* 18 (1972): 224–86.

Ferster, Judith. "Interpretation and Imitation in Chaucer's Franklin's Tale." In *Medieval Literature: Criticism, Ideology and History.* Ed. David Aers. Brighton: Harvester Press, 1986. 148–68.

Foucault, Michel. "Space, Knowledge and Power." In *The Foucault Reader.* Ed. Paul Rabinow. New York: Pantheon Books, 1984. 239–56.

Frank, Roberta. "*Beowulf* and Sutton Hoo: The Odd Couple." In *Voyage to the Other World.* Ed. Calvin B. Kendall and Peter S. Wells. Minneapolis: University of Minnesota Press, 1992. 47–64.

Frantzen, Allen J. "Prologue: Documents and Monuments: Difference and Interdisciplinarity in the Study of Medieval Culture." In *Speaking Two Languages: Traditional Disciplines and Contemporary Theory in Medieval Studies.* Ed. Allen J. Frantzen. Albany: State University of New York Press, 1991. 1–33.

———. *Desire for Origins: New Language, Old English, and Teaching the Tradition.* New Brunswick: Rutgers University Press, 1990.

Gandelman, Claude. *Reading Pictures, Viewing Texts.* Bloomington: Indiana University Press, 1991.

Works Cited

Gardner, Helen. "Clive Staples Lewis." *The Proceedings of the British Academy* 51 (1965): 417–28.

Garmonsway, G. N., Jacqueline Simpson, and Hilda Ellis Davidson. *Beowulf and Its Analogues.* London: Dent, 1968.

Gilchrist, Roberta. "The Spatial Archaeology of Gender Domains: A Case Study of Medieval Nunneries." *Archaeological Review from Cambridge* 7, no. 1 (1988): 21–28.

Glob, P. V. *The Bog People: Iron Age Man Preserved.* Trans. R. L. S. Bruce-Mitford. London: Granada, 1971.

Goffart, Walter. "Hetware and Hugas: Datable Anachronisms in Beowulf." In *The Dating of Beowulf.* Ed. Colin Chase. Toronto: University of Toronto Press, 1981. 83–100.

Grágás. See *Laws of Early Iceland.*

Grænlendinga Saga. Trans. Magnus Magnusson and Hermann Pálsson. In *The Vinland Sagas: The Norse Discovery of America.* Harmondsworth: Penguin, 1965.

Gravdal, Kathryn. *Ravishing Maidens: Writing Rape in Medieval French Literature and Law.* Philadelphia: University of Pennsylvania Press, 1991.

———. "Camouflaging Rape: The Rhetoric of Sexual Violence in the Medieval Pastourelle." *Romanic Review* 76, no. 4 (1985): 361–73.

Grettir's Saga. Trans. Denton Fox and Hermann Pálsson. Toronto: University of Toronto Press, 1974.

Grettis Saga Ásmundarsonar, Bandamannasaga, Odds, Þáttr Ofeigsonar. Ed. Guðni Jónsson. Íslensk Fornrít, vol. 7. Reykjavik: Íslenzka Fornrítafélag, 1936.

Haigh, Daniel H. *The Anglo-Saxon Sagas: An Examination of Their Value as Aids to History.* London: John Russell Smith, 1861.

Hastrup, Kirsten. "Tracing the Tradition: An Anthropological Perspective on *Grettissaga Asmundarsonar.*" In *Structure and Meaning in Old Norse Literature.* Ed. John Lindow, Lars Lönnroth, and Gerd Wolfgang Weber. Odense: Odense University Press, 1986. 281–313.

———. *Culture and History in Medieval Iceland.* Oxford: Clarendon Press, 1985.

Haywood, John. *Dark Age Naval Power: A Reassessment of Frankish and Anglo-Saxon Activity.* London: Routledge, 1991.

Heimskringla. See Snorri Sturluson.

Henrikson, Alf. *Svenska Historia.* 2 vols. Stockholm: Bonnier, 1966.

Hight, G. A., trans. *The Saga of Grettir the Strong.* London: Dent, 1914.

Hrolf Kraki's Saga. In *Eirik the Red and Other Icelandic Sagas.* Trans. Gwyn Jones. London: Oxford University Press, 1961.

Huppé, Bernard F. *The Hero in the Earthly City: A Reading of Beowulf.* Binghamton: SUNY Medieval and Renaissance Texts and Studies, 1984.

Huyshe, Wentworth. *Beowulf: An Old English Epic.* London: Routledge, 1907.

Iceland Road Guide. Ed. Örlygur Hálfdánarson. Reykjavik: Örn og Örlygur HF, 1981.

Ives, Jack D. "Landscape Change and Human Response during a Thousand Years of Climatic Fluctuation and Volcanism: Skaftafell, Southeast Iceland." *Pirineos* 137 (1991): 5–50.

Jameson, Fredric. "Spatial Equivalents: Post-Modern Architecture and the World System." In *The States of "Theory": History, Art, and Critical Discourse.* Ed. David Carroll. New York: Columbia University Press, 1990. 125–48.

Jesch, Judith. *Women in the Viking Age.* Woodbridge: Boydell Press, 1991.

Jochens, Jenny. "The Medieval Icelandic Heroine: Fact or Fiction?" *Viator* 17 (1986): 35–50.

Jones, Gwyn. *A History of the Vikings.* 2d ed. Oxford: Oxford University Press, 1984.

Karras, Ruth Mazo. *Slavery and Society in Medieval Scandinavia.* New Haven: Yale University Press, 1988.

Kendall, Calvin B., and Peter S. Wells, eds. *Voyage to the Other World: The Legacy of Sutton Hoo.* Minneapolis: University of Minnesota Press, 1992.

Kolodny, Annette. *The Land before Her: Fantasy and Experience of the American Frontiers, 1630–1860*. Chapel Hill: University of North Carolina Press, 1984.

———. *The Lay of the Land: Metaphor as Experience and History in American Life and Letters*. Chapel Hill: University of North Carolina Press, 1975.

Landnámabók. See *The Book of Settlements*.

The Laws of Early Iceland: Grágás. Trans. Andrew Dennis, Peter Foote, and Richard Perkins. Winnipeg: University of Manitoba Press, 1980.

Laxdæla Saga. Trans. Magnus Magnusson and Hermann Pálsson. Harmondsworth: Penguin, 1969.

Leake, Jane Acomb. *The Geats of Beowulf*. Madison: University of Wisconsin Press, 1967.

Lefkowitz, Mary R. "The New Cults of the Goddess." *The American Scholar* 62 (Spring, 1993): 261–68.

Le Guin, Ursula. "Sur." In *The Compass Rose*. Toronto: Bantam, 1983. 253–71.

Lincoff, Gary, and D. H. Mitchell, M.D. *Toxic and Hallucinogenic Mushroom Poisoning: A Handbook for Physicians and Mushroom Hunters*. New York: Van Nostrand Reinhold Company, 1977.

Liuzza, Roy M. "The Year's Work in Old English Studies." *Old English Newsletter* 24, no. 2 (Winter 1991): 30–36.

Lopez, Barry. *Crossing Open Ground*. New York: Scribner, 1988.

———. *Arctic Dreams: Imagination and Desire in a Northern Landscape*. New York: Scribner, 1986.

Lowenthal, David. "Age and Artifact: Dilemmas of Appreciation." In *The Interpretation of Ordinary Landscapes*. Ed. D. W. Meinig. Oxford: Oxford University Press, 1979. 103–28.

Lund, Niels, ed. *Two Voyagers at the Court of King Alfred: The Ventures of Ohthere and Wulfstan Together with the Description of Northern Europe from the Old English Orosius*. Trans. Christine E. Fell. York: William Sessions, Ltd., 1984.

Mackay, Donnie. "Images in a Landscape: Bonnie Prince Charlie and the Highland Clearances." In *Writing the Past in the Present*. Ed. Frederick Baker and Julian Thomas. Lampeter: Saint David's University, 1990. 192–203.

Magoun, F. P. "The Geography of Hygelac's Raid on the Lands of the West Frisians and the Haettware, ca. 530 A.D." *English Studies* 34 (1953): 160–63.

Marcus, G. J. *The Conquest of the North Atlantic*. Woodbridge: D. S. Brewer, 1980.

McGrail, Sean, ed. *Maritime Celts, Frisians and Saxons: Papers Presented to a Conference at Oxford*. London: Council for British Archaeology, 1990.

Meinig, D. W., ed. *The Interpretation of Ordinary Landscapes: Geographical Essays*. Oxford: Oxford University Press, 1979.

Miller, Jim Wayne. "Anytime the Ground Is Uneven: The Outlook for Regional Studies and What to Look Out For." In *Geography and Literature: A Meeting of the Disciplines*. Ed. William E. Mallory and Paul Simpson-Housley. Syracuse: Syracuse University Press, 1987. 1–20.

Modéer, Ivar. "Windholm och Vëderö." *Namn och Bygd* 20 (1932): 138–46.

Monk, Janice. "Approaches to the Study of Women and Landscape." *Environmental Review* 8, no. 1 (Spring 1984): 23–33.

Montelius, Oscar. *Böhuslänska Fornsaker fran Hednatiden*. Tredje Häftet. Stockholm: P. A. Norstedt & Söner, 1880.

Moore, Henrietta. *Space, Text and Gender: An Anthropological Study of the Marakwet of Kenya*. Cambridge: Cambridge University Press, 1986.

Njal's Saga. Trans. Magnus Magnusson and Hermann Pálsson. Harmondsworth: Penguin, 1960.

Osborn, Marijane. " 'Verbal Sea-Charts' and Beowulf's Approach to Denmark." In *De Gustibus: Essays for Alain Renoir*. Ed. John Miles Foley. New York: Garland, 1992. 441–55.

———. "Beowulf's Landfall in *Finna Land.*" *Neuphilologische Mitteilungen* 90 (1989): 137–42.

———. *Beowulf: A Verse Translation with Treasures of the Ancient North.* Berkeley: University of California Press, 1983.

Overing, Gillian R. "Recent Writing on Old English: A Response." *Æstel* 1 (April 1993): 135–49.

———. *Language, Sign and Gender in "Beowulf."* Carbondale, Ill.: University of Southern Illinois Press, 1990.

———. "Reinventing Beowulf's Voyage to Denmark." *Old English Newsletter* 21, no. 2 (Spring 1988): 30–39.

———. "Some Aspects of Metonymy in Old English Poetry." *Concerning Poetry* 19 (1986): 1–20.

Patterson, Lee. *Negotiating the Past: The Historical Understanding of Medieval Literature.* Madison: University of Wisconsin Press, 1987.

Piehler, Paul. *The Visionary Landscape: A Study in Medieval Allegory.* London: Edward Arnold, 1971.

Pocock, Douglas C. D., ed. *Humanistic Geography and Literature: Essays on the Experience of Place.* London: Croom Helm, 1981.

Pratt, Mary Louise. "Fieldwork in Common Places." In *Writing Culture.* Ed. James Clifford and George E. Marcus. Berkeley: University of California Press, 1986. 27–50.

Rabinowitz, Peter J. "Assertion and Assumption: Fictional Patterns and the External World." *Publications of the Modern Language Association* 96 (1981): 408–19.

Ricoeur, Paul. *The Reality of the Historical Past.* Milwaukee: Marquette University Press, 1984.

Robinson, F. C. "Beowulf." In *The Cambridge Companion to Old English Literature.* Ed. Malcolm Godden and Michael Lapidge. Cambridge: Cambridge University Press, 1991. 142–59.

———. "The Prescient Woman in Old English Literature." In *Philologia Anglica: Festschrift for Professor Y. Terasawa.* Tokyo: Kenkyusha, 1988. 241–50.

———. "Teaching the Backgrounds: History, Religion, Culture." In *Approaches to Teaching Beowulf.* Ed. Jess B. Bessinger, Jr., and Robert T. Yeager. New York: MLA Press, 1984. 107–22.

———. "Elements of the Marvellous in the Characterization of Beowulf: A Reconsideration of the Textual Evidence." In *Old English Studies in Honor of John C. Pope.* Ed. Robert B. Burlin and Edward B. Irving. Toronto: University of Toronto Press, 1974. 119–37.

———. "Beowulf's Retreat from Frisia: Some Textual Problems in ll. 2361–2362." *Studies in Philology* 62 (1965): 1–16.

Roesdahl, Else. "Princely Burial in Scandinavia at the Time of the Conversion." In *Voyage to the Other World.* Ed. Calvin B. Kendall and Peter S. Wells. Minneapolis: University of Minnesota Press, 1992. 155–70.

Ross, Margaret Clunies. *Long Echoes: Old Norse Myths in Medieval Icelandic Society.* Forthcoming from Odense University Press.

Russell, Bertrand. *The Autobiography of Bertrand Russell: 1914–1944.* Boston: Little, Brown, 1967.

Sarrazin, Gregor. *Beowulf-Studien.* Berlin: Mayer & Müller, 1888.

Saxo Grammaticus. *A History of the Danes.* Ed. H. E. Davidson. Cambridge: D. S. Brewer, 1979.

Shippey, Thomas. Review of Jesse Byock's *Medieval Iceland.* In *The London Review of Books,* 11, no. 11 (June 1989): 16–17.

Sisam, Kenneth. "The Anglo-Saxon Royal Genealogies." *Publications of the British Archaeological Society* 39 (1953): 287–348.

Smyser, H. M. "Ibn Fadlan's Account of the Rus, with Some Commentary and Some Allusions to *Beowulf.*" In *Medieval and Linguistic Studies in Honor of Francis Peabody*

Magoun, Jr. Ed. Jess B. Bessinger, Jr., and Robert P. Creed. London: Allen and Unwin, 1965. 92–119.

Snorri Sturluson. *Edda.* Trans. Anthony Faulkes. London: Dent, 1987.

———. *Egil's Saga.* Trans. Hermann Pálsson and Paul Edwards. Harmondsworth: Penguin, 1976.

———. *Heimskringla: History of the Kings of Norway.* Trans. Lee M. Hollander. Austin: University of Texas Press, 1964.

Stanley, E. G. "The Date of *Beowulf:* Some Doubts and No Conclusions." In *The Dating of Beowulf.* Ed. Colin Chase. Toronto: University of Toronto Press, 1981. 197–211.

Starcke, Viggo. *Denmark in World History.* Philadelphia: University of Pennsylvania Press, 1962.

Steblin-Kamenskii, M. I. *The Saga Mind.* Trans. Kenneth H. Ober. Odense: Odense University Press, 1973.

Stitt, J. Michael. *Beowulf and the Bear's Son: Epic, Saga, and Fairytale in Northern Germanic Tradition.* New York: Garland, 1992.

Stjerna, Knut Martin. *Essays on Questions Connected with the Old English Poem of Beowulf.* Ed. and trans. John R. Clark Hall. Coventry: Curtis and Beamish, 1912.

Storms, Godfrid. "The Significance of Hygelac's Raid." *Nottingham Medieval Studies* 14 (1970): 4–9.

Ströker, Elisabeth. *Investigations in Philosophy of Space.* Trans. Algis Mickunas. Athens, Ohio: Ohio University Press, 1987.

Swaney, Deanna. *Iceland, Greenland and the Faroe Islands: A Travel Survival Kit.* Hawthorne, Australia: Lonely Planet Publications, 1991.

Swanton, Michael, ed. and trans. *Beowulf.* Manchester: Manchester University Press, 1978.

Swearer, Randolph, Raymond Oliver, and Marijane Osborn. *Beowulf: A Likeness.* New Haven: Yale University Press, 1990.

Sweet, Henry. *Sweet's Anglo-Saxon Reader in Prose and Verse.* 14th ed. Revised by C. T. Onions. Oxford: Clarendon Press, 1959.

Tacitus. *On Britain and Germany.* Trans. H. Mattingly. Revised by S. A. Handford. Harmondsworth: Penguin, 1970.

Thomas, Julian. "Same, Other, Analogue: Writing the Past." In *Writing the Past in the Present.* Ed. Frederick Baker and Julian Thomas. Lampeter: Saint David's University, 1990. 18–23.

Tolkien, J. R. R. *Finn and Hengest: The Fragment and the Episode.* Ed. Alan Bliss. London: Allen and Unwin, 1982.

Traill, David. "Schliemann's Discovery of 'Priam's Treasure': A Re-Examination of the Evidence." *Journal of Hellenic Studies* 104 (1984): 96–115.

Tripp, Raymond P., Jr. "Lingworms and Lies: Three New *Beowulf* Books." *In Geardagum* 11 (June 1990): 73–87.

Tuan, Yi-Fu. "Geographical Theory: Queries from a Cultural Geographer." *Geographical Analysis* 15, no. 1 (January 1983): 69–72.

———. "Thought and Landscape: The Eye and the Mind's Eye." In *The Interpretation of Ordinary Landscapes.* Ed. D. W. Meinig. Oxford: Oxford University Press, 1979. 89–102.

———. *Space and Place: The Perspective of Experience.* Minneapolis: University of Minnesota Press, 1977.

———. "Geopiety: A Theme in Man's Attachment to Nature and Place." In *Geographies of the Mind.* Ed. David Lowenthal and Martyn J. Bowden. New York: Oxford University Press, 1976. 11–39.

———. "Geography, Phenomenology, and the Study of Human Nature." *Canadian Geographer* 15, no. 3 (1971): 181–92.

Vita S. Luidgeri. Ed. G. H. Pertz. *Monumenta Germaniae Historica,* Scriptores 2. Hanover: Hahn, 1829. 403–29.

Wadstein, Elis. "The Beowulf Poem as an English National Epos." *Acta Philologica Scandinavica* 8 (1933): 273–91.

Waterson, Roxanna. *The Living House.* Oxford: Oxford University Press, 1990.

Whitelock, Dorothy. *The Audience of Beowulf.* Oxford: Clarendon, 1951.

Wilson, Allan C., and Rebecca L. Cann. "The Recent African Genesis of Humans." *Scientific American* 267 (April 1992): 68–73. [For an opposing view, see *Scientific American* 267: 76–79, and also Philip E. Ross, "Shaking the Tree: Will Statistical Analysis of DNA Pinpoint Human Origins?" *Scientific American* 267 (December 1992): 36–38.]

Wollstonecraft, Mary. *Letters Written during a Short Residence in Sweden, Norway and Denmark.* Lincoln and London: University of Nebraska Press, 1976.

Woolf, Henry B. "The Name of Beowulf." *Englische Studien* 72 (1937): 7–9.

Wrenn, C. L. "Recent Work on *Beowulf* to 1956." Appendix to *Beowulf: An Introduction.* By R. W. Chambers. Cambridge: Cambridge University Press, 1963. 504–48.

———, ed. *Beowulf with the Finnesburg Fragment.* London: George G. Harrap, Ltd., 1958.

Wurmius, Olaus. *Danicorum Monumentorum Libri Sex.* Hafniae (Copenhagen): I. Moltkenium, 1643.

Wylie, Jonathan, and David Margolin. *The Ring of Dancers: Images of Faroese Culture.* Philadelphia: University of Pennsylvania Press, 1981.

Zimmerman, Michael. "Feminism, Deep Ecology, and Environmental Ethics." *Environmental Ethics* 9 (Spring 1987): 21–44.

Index

Compiled by Eileen Quam and Theresa Wolner

Index

times and distances, 3; on verbal sea charts, 11; on Viking ships, 120n
Cultural geography, 42

Dale of Shadows (Iceland), 106, 109
Damico, Helen, 69
Dayraven (Hygelac's slayer), 32
"Dead reckoning," 10
Denmark: origins of name, 120n; setting sail from, xvi. *See also* Wedermark
Desio, Ardito, 89
Dewey, John, 42–43, 48
Displacement, 79, 85
Distance: conceptions of, 49–50
Domarring, 31
Dragons, 30–31
Dragsmark, 30, 120n
Drangey (Iceland): as home to Grettir, 68; journey to, xxii, 92, *96*, 95–118; otherness of, 106; video of, 99–100, 110; view from Fagranes, *72*, 108, 109; view from Hegranes, *72*; view from Reykir, *102*. *See also plates 7–14*

Eadgils the Geat, 33
Ecgtheow, 9
Ecology: and feminism, 47
Egeria, xxi–xxii
Egil's Saga, 19, 53, 55
Eiriksson, Jon, 98–104 passim, 107–13 passim, 118
Ekborg, Jan, 29–30, 36
Elsinore (Denmark), 16. *See also* Helsingör
Experience: and theory, xvi

Fagranes (Iceland), 98, 99, 107, 108, 109
Fagraskogafell (Iceland), 97, *plate 2*
Fairhair, Harold, 25, 51
Falkenberg (Sweden), 8, 10
Faroe Islands (Denmark), xviii
Farrell, R. T.: on Gautar, 34; on Geats as Gautar, 2; on Iron Age treasures, 25
Feminism: and critique of heroism, 103; and ecology, 47; and psychology, 75–76
Ferster, Judith, 36
Feuds, 64; inheritance of, 44
Fiction: and audience, 90; historicizing, xiii
Fin: as place-name element, 29
Finmarken (Norway), 27
Finnheden (Sweden), 27, 29
Finnsburg, xx
Fjällbacka (Sweden), 7, 8, 34, 36
Forest, 71

Frantzen, Allen, xiv, 119n
Freawaru, 20
Frisians, 27
Frontier: in Iceland, 47, 50–51, 71, 76; and women in place, 47, 76, 125n

Galtaback (Sweden), 8
Gammel Lejre (Denmark): as archaeological site, 12–13, 18, 19, 21, 23; journey to, 2, 12; location of, 2, 18. *See also* Heorot; Leire; Lejre; Roskilde
Gandelman, Claude, 14
Gardner, Helen, 42
Gaut Elf River, 25
Gautar: cultural identity of, 34; domination by Svear, 34; Geats as, xx, 2, 15, 25, 119n; homeland of, 14; port city of, 3; in Sweden, 34. *See also* Geats
Gautland, 25
Geatas, 14. *See also* Gautar
Geatland, 26, 27
Geats: as Gautar, xx, 2, 15, 25, 119n; historicity of, 15, 122–23n; as Jutes, xx, 121n; location of, xx, 14–15, 25–27, *26*; as mythical, 14; port city of, 3; and Roskilde Fjord, 12; sailing expertise of, 10; in southwest Sweden, xx; vs. Swedes, 33; treasure burials, *26*; voyages of, 15–18 passim, 22, 24–25. *See also* Gautar
Gender: and sense of space, 44–45, 76–77
Geopiety, 8, 52, 58
Germania (Tacitus), 19
Germanic peoples, 19, 34
Gilbjerg Hoved, 17
Gisli, 98
Glaciers, 30
Glam: Grettir's fight with, 67, 106, 109, 117
Glaum, 110
Glob, P. V., 121n
Glomma River (Sweden), 24, 27. *See also* Raum River
Gódafoss waterfalls (Iceland), 41, *plate 5*
Goddesses: as Eve, 107; presence of, 105
Göta Älv river (Sweden), 3, 8, 24, 27
Göteborg (Sweden): exploring, 29; as port city, 3; sailing from, 4, 8, 25; sailing to, 6, 7
Gotland (Sweden): island; as homeland, 14
Götland (Sweden): mainland, Geats in, 25
Grænlendinga Saga, 76
Grave markers, 56

Index

Oral maps: and *Beowulf*'s landscapes, 17;
and landfall approaches, 11; of naviga-
tional knowledge, 10
Orust (Sweden), 8
Oslo (Norway), 27
Oslo Fjord (Sweden), 6
Osvifsdottir, Gudrun. *See* Gudrun
Otherness: of attuned space, 118; of
Drangey, 106; and ritual, 20
Outlawry: in medieval Iceland, 64, 68, 71

Past: life of, xiii; negotiation with, xvii,
119n; and present, xiii-xiv, xviii, xxi, 8;
re-creating/reinventing, xiii, xiv; study
of, xiv; versions of, xiv
Patterson, Lee:, 119n
*Pilgrimage to the Saga-Steads of Iceland,
A* (Collingwood and Stefánsson), 41
Place: as catalyst, xvi; experience of, xv,
xvii; feasibility of, 18; fictional in literature, 15; and gender, 44–45, 76–77; in
Iceland, 41, 46, 47, 48–55; interrogation
of, 88–89; locating, xvi; metonymic
relationship to, 89–93; and narration,
44; nature of, xvi, 63–64; as negotiative
activity, xiv, 104; orientation to, xx;
perception of, xxi; power of, xiii, xiv,
46, 53; as process, xvii, 42; self in, 41,
43–46, 64–79; sense of, 8, 42; translating, 79–93; unitary definitions of, xvi;
the wild as, 72–73; women's relation to,
44–45, 47. *See also* Homeland;
Landscape; Translocation
Pocock, D. C. D., 42
Poetry: Latin American, 81–82; and place,
81–82
Pratt, Mary Louise, xvii, xxi

Queen Modthryth, 103

Rabinowitz, Peter, 90
Raíz Salvaje (Ibarbourou), 81
Ranríki, 24, 35
Rape: by Grettir, 45, 102, 123–24n
Raum River (Sweden), 24, 27, 29, 122n. *See
also* Glomma River
Raumaríki (Norway), 27
Reality of the Historical Past, The
(Ricoeur), 119n
Reinvention: and conjecture, 3; process of,
1; results of, 13; use of term, 2
Religious conception: and law in medieval
Iceland, 50

Reykir (Iceland): farms, 107; Grettir's swim
to, 101, 109, 115; horse ride to, 103; hot
springs, 102; view of Drangey from, 98,
102
Reykjavik (Iceland), xiv, 96, 97, 98, 106,
107
Ricoeur, Paul, 119n
Rímbegla, 3
Ring of Dancers, The (Wylie and Margolin),
xviii, xix-xx
Ritual, 20
Robinson, Fred C., 34
Rock carvings: at Bohuslän, 7–8; at Hög
Edsten, 31
Romeriki (Norway), 27
Roskilde (Denmark): as cathedral town, 18;
fjords leading to, 16–17; place-name, 21;
sailing from, 13; sailing to, 9, 11, 12; as
Scylding Danes' location, 2, 16, 21. *See
also* Gammel Lejre
Roskilde Fjord (Denmark), 12, 17
Roskilde Museum (Denmark), 21
Ross, Margaret Clunies, 124n
Russell, Bertrand, 116

Sacrificial bog, 18–19
Saga Mind, The (Steblin-Kamenskii), 65
Sagasteads: sketches of, xxi
Sailing times and distances, 2–3, 4; mea-
surement of a day's sailing, 2–3
Saint Augustine: on medieval texts, 36
Sarrazin, Gregor: on dragons, 30; on
Finnsland, 29; on geography of *Beowulf*,
21, 22, 29; on Lejre, 21
Saudarkrokur (Iceland), 108, 109, 111, 112
Saxo Grammaticus, 21
Sciringesheal (Norway), 4, 8
Scylding Danes: battles, 20; location of, 2,
14; royal hall of, 14, 16
Seamanship: Norse, 10, 11, 16, 53–54
Sejerø (Denmark), 13
Self: and community in Iceland, 51; and
place, 43–46; and place in Iceland, 41
Sex ratio: in settlement Iceland, 76
Seydisfjord (Iceland), 35
Shakespeare, William, 16, 17
Ship funerals, 20, 121–22n
Ship-setting, 20
Shipbuilding, 53–54
Skagafjord (Iceland), 95, 98, 99, 104, 107,
108
Skålberg, 30
Skallagrim's grave (Iceland), 55–56, *56*, 58

139

Index

Widsith (poem), 18, 19, 20
Wife of Bath, xxii
Wiglaf, 31
Wild: as place, 72–73
Wilde, Oscar, 42
Williams, Raymond, 46
Wollstonecraft, Mary, xxi
Women: and frontier, 47, 76, 125n; in
    Icelandic culture, 76–77, 124n; relation
    to place, 44–45, 47, 69, 73–74, 124–25n;
    restraints on, 74, 76; saga journeys of,
    xxi-xxii

Wordsworth, William, 42–43, 47
Wormius, Olaus, 19
Wrenn, C. L., 3, 27
Writing the Past in the Present (Thomas),
    xiii-xiv, 119n
Wulfstan: as coastal sailor, 3; voyages of, 4
Wylie, Jonathan, xviii

Ynglinga Saga, 20, 33

Zealand (Denmark): cliffs of, 17; homeland
    near, 14, 16; sailing from, 4; sailing to
    coast of, 9, 10, 11

Gillian R. Overing is professor of English at Wake Forest University, where she teaches Old and Middle English, linguistics, and women's studies, and coordinates the Medieval Studies program. In addition to articles on Old English literature, literary history, and contemporary theory, she has coedited *Teaching Writing: Pedagogy, Gender, and Equity* and *Class and Gender in Early English Literature,* and is the author of *Language, Sign, and Gender in "Beowulf."*

After holding lectureships or fellowships at universities in England, Scotland, Northern Ireland, Alaska, Hawaii, and Iceland, **Marijane Osborn** now teaches and is the current director of the Medieval Studies program at the University of California at Davis. She has authored or coauthored three books on *Beowulf* and one on runes, and has published numerous articles, poems, and translations.